THE *Mermaid* & THE *Lobster Diver*

GENDER, SEXUALITY, AND MONEY ON THE MISKITO COAST

LAURA HOBSON HERLIHY

University of New Mexico Press

Albuquerque

© 2012 by the University of New Mexico Press
All rights reserved. Published 2012
Printed in the United States of America

17   16   15   14   13   12   1   2   3   4   5   6

LIBRARY OF CONGRESS CATALOGING-IN-PUBLICATION DATA

Herlihy, Laura Hobson, 1962–
The mermaid and the lobster diver : gender, sexuality, and money on the Miskito coast /
Laura Hobson Herlihy.
    p. cm.
Includes bibliographical references and index.
ISBN 978-0-8263-5093-0 (pbk. : alk. paper) — ISBN 978-0-8263-5094-7 (electronic)
1. Miskito Indians—Social conditions. 2. Miskito Indians—Economic conditions.
3. Miskito Indians—Sexual behavior. 4. Social structure—Mosquitia (Nicaragua
and Honduras) 5. Matrilineal kinship—Mosquitia (Nicaragua and Honduras)
6. Lobster industry—Mosquitia (Nicaragua and Honduras) 7. Sexual division of
labor—Mosquitia (Nicaragua and Honduras) 8. Mosquitia (Nicaragua and
Honduras)—Social conditions. 9. Mosquitia (Nicaragua and Honduras)—
Economic conditions. I. Title.
F1529.M9H47 2012
972.85004′97882—dc23

                        2011051673

DESIGN AND LAYOUT: Melissa Tandysh
Composed in 10.25/14 Minion Pro Regular
Display type is Incognito Regular

Contents

Figures, Maps, and Tables

Maps

Tables

Acknowledgments

I would like to thank several influential professors for guiding my interest in cultural anthropology. I discovered anthropology as an undergraduate at Tulane University, when I attended college in my hometown of New Orleans. I took practically every class offered by Mayan linguist Judy Maxwell, who ignited my passion for indigenous language and culture. After graduating I attended a William and Mary ethnographic field school in the Caribbean where I worked with Eric Ayisi and studied matrifocality. In Louisiana State University's master's program in anthropology, my MA advisor was Mayan linguist Jill Brody, and I traveled through Mexico with Robert West, William Davidson, and Miles Richardson before beginning my master's field research in central Mexico. During this pivotal moment in my life, I also met my husband, geographer Peter Herlihy, who became not only a mentor and colleague but also my lifetime partner and the father of our two growing children, Simone and Hobbs. Peter first brought me to the Miskito Coast on an ersatz honeymoon, and it is him to whom I dedicate the book.

During my doctoral studies at the University of Kansas (KU), I was lucky to work with John Janzen, my dissertation advisor, who also guided my understanding of the African dimensions of the Caribbean; with Elizabeth Kuznesof, who situated my interest in family and gender within greater Latin America; and with Charles Stansifer, who brought to life the unique history of the Caribbean coast of Central America. While at KU I garnered two research grants, from the Fulbright and Tinker Foundations (through the KU Center of Latin American Studies), which generously supported my doctoral field research. I also benefited from ongoing conversations with fellow graduate students who studied the Miskito Coast, such as Derek Smith, Ratna Radakrishna, David Cochran, and especially Elmor Wood, a Miskitu geographer who made his way to the University of Kansas. Silvia González Carias, a Honduran anthropologist, also completed KU's master's program in anthropology and added to the dynamic group of students. Silvia returned to KU as a visiting Fulbright scholar in spring 2011 and helped me teach a class on Miskitu language and culture.

Only through the kindness of the people of Kuri could this book come to fruition. In Kuri, Kuka Denecela adopted me as one of her daughters, and Delfina, Enemecia, Tomasa, and Ilabia treated me as a sister. Delfina especially took me under her wing to reveal the dynamic social and economic role of women on the coast. Siksto George, Delfina's husband, made sure we were safe, while their children and other members of the community incorporated Peter and me into their daily lives and made us feel at home. Alan, Rolins, Daugoberto, Nela, Marta, Tangni, Berihilda, Lyvian, Gladys, Nora, Dina, Mis Dina, Elbecina, Olda, Tomasita, Doralicet, Yanali, Rustelia, Mario, Bujeron, Marcos, Trit, Rosie, Elbecina, and Opni: thank you all for the fun memories. When I returned to Kuri in August 2010, those in the village insisted that they wanted their real names to appear in the final writing of the book. For this reason, I am using their real names.

In Tegucigalpa I had the support of the Honduran Museum of History and Anthropology and benefited from my interactions with archaeologist George Hasemann, historian Gloria Lara Pinto, and anthropologists Silvia González Carias and Fernando Cruz. I also was helped by MOPAWI, a development organization working in Moskitia, and especially by Osvaldo Mungia and Aldalberto Padilla. I owe a great deal to the insights of David Dodds, who completed his doctoral research in anthropology in the neighboring town of Belén, and to Nicaraguan linguist Danilo Salamanca, for giving me my first Miskitu grammar. A special thanks also goes out to Philip Dennis, an expert on Miskitu culture, for giving my manuscript a critical reading and for his thoughtful editorial comments, and to Mary Helms for her inspiring work among the Miskitu peoples in Asang.

Last and perhaps most importantly, I want to thank my family, especially my parents, Jane and Neal Hobson, for supporting my education and encouraging me to follow my interests, which were not of the ordinary. My father, Neal, passed away before this book was published, and we all miss his guidance and love. Aunt Tita, cousin Catherine, sisters Ellie and Lisa, brothers Neal and Gordon, and of course, my children, Simone and Hobbs, have all in their own way been a part of this book.

Introduction

Washed Ashore / A Seaside View

To reach the village of Kuri we flew from La Ceiba to Palacios, crossed Ibans Lagoon to Cocobila in a tuk-tuk, and then walked overland for an hour and a half on a savannah path between lagoon and sea. The path continued through a tunnel of sea grapes before spitting us out on a white Caribbean beach. Walking past Tampa Tingni Lagoon, we could see Kuri perched on a sand bluff; the village looked friendly, with green grass cut tight to the ground, smoke effusing from the cookhouses, and coconut trees waving in the sea breeze. We entered Kuri's central cluster of houses and set our backpacks down on the ground. A kuka, or grandmother, stepped out of her home to greet me and my geographer husband.

Kuka Denecela sported a light-blue turban fashioned from a towel twisted around her head. More than a dozen beaded necklaces graced her neck. Spreading her arms wide, she spoke. "Bien . . . ," she false started. "Bienvenidos . . . a . . . Kuri." She dropped her arms and exhaled audibly, as if exhausted from having to speak in Spanish, a second language to her indigenous Miskitu.

"Vé aquellos arboles?" (See those trees?) She pointed with her lips perched toward the edge of the yard. "Son mios . . . y este es mi patio." (They are mine . . . and this is my patio.) She glided her hand slowly through the air to frame the yard. "Vé

aquellas casas?" (See those houses?) "Son de mis hijas. . . . Las doy tierra para que vivan cerca de mi." (They're my daughters.' . . . I give them land so they can stay close to me.) After pausing a moment to view the social landscape, she lip-pointed to a nearby house. "Ustedes pueden quedar allá mientras mi hija Enemecia esta trabajando en el río." (You can stay there while my daughter Enemecia is upriver tending the fields).

An auspicious beginning, I thought to myself. Here I was, a neophyte ethnographer hoping to study female-centered social organization, and within the first few minutes in Kuri the head of a matrilocal group, the *kuka* herself, offered me and my husband one of her daughters' homes. Peter and I settled in by nightfall, unpacking enough for a comfortable night's sleep. The next day we cleaned the house, organized our sparse possessions, and arranged to live in Enemecia's house for six months.

Kuri's houses were thatched-roof, one-room structures with wooden walls and floors. The houses were built on posts, elevated three to five feet from the ground. Raised houses were an attempt to keep villagers dry during the wet season. Most houses had a separate cookhouse nearby, built directly on the ground with a *fogón*, or clay hearth, inside. A few of the larger houses were painted light blue beneath a tin roof, a local sign of prosperity. Less substantial structures with bamboo walls sat on the ground and distinguished the poorer residents. Dooryard gardens of breadfruit, orange, mango, cashew, and berry trees were cultivated around the permanent houses.

Everyone in the family referred to Delfina as "Kikalmuk" (the Miskitu kinship term for eldest sister) or just "Kikal." Delfina was Kuka Denecela's first child, born to a Creole father (Creoles maintained a higher socioeconomic ranking than the Miskitu). She was, by far, the most well off of the sisters, especially given that the other sisters' father, Octavio Ferrera, was a Miskitu man of considerably lesser economic means.

As a girl Delfina had lived in her Creole aunt Sara's house in Brus Lakun (Brewer's Lagoon), the largest Miskitu town in Honduras. In Brus she helped Aunt Sara with domestic chores and eventually met and married Siksto George (literally, George VI), one of the first Miskitu elementary teachers in Honduras. Siksto was originally from Auka, Nicaragua, and after finishing his teaching stint in Brus Lakun, he followed Delfina back to her home community of Kuri, where he worked for twenty years in the neighboring village of Utla Almuk. In a region where the majority of men worked as deepwater lobster divers and farmers, Siksto stood out as one of the few professionals.[1] He also distinguished himself as the de facto male leader of Kuri, as the most visible and educated of the four men in permanent residence. Other men in permanent residence included a pastor and two elderly men who no longer worked their fields.

Delfina inherited coastal village property and agricultural and hunting lands upriver from her mother's side of the family. She not only had garnered the family's coveted beachfront property to build her home but she also benefitted from Siksto's steady salary as a teacher. The couple later built and opened a small comedor (restaurant) and bodega (small store). Claiming only one biological child, their family grew through successive adoptions of Delfina's younger sisters' children. Within a few years their home had expanded into a compound, including a sleeping house, a separate cookhouse, a bathing house, and the comedor and bodega. Delfina and Siksto later began working with an ecotourism company from Tegucigalpa that catered to North American and European tourists. This business connection prompted them to build a house for ecotourists to rent by the night. Newer and larger beachfront homes soon followed for their biological and adopted children.

Two other sisters—Tomasa and Ilabia—had their houses nearby. Tomasa's house sat on four-foot posts with a crooked staircase in front that climbed straight up the middle. Tomasa was a single mom with eight children who ran up and down the steps incessantly; she reminded me of the lady who lived in the shoe. Ilabia's home, small and lower to the ground, was a cottage that did not provide enough space for her four children. The children preferred to stay nights with Delfina. The cottage-house was deserted during our time in Kuri, as Ilabia had separated from her husband, Mindel, a carpenter and lobster diver. Their children were thereafter raised permanently by Delfina.

The house where we lived was vacated due to a similar situation. Enemecia had recently separated from her husband, Alan, a former biosphere reserve park ranger turned private guide. Alan had returned to his mother's matrigroup in Tasbapauni, and Enemecia took her five children (one from her first union, three with Alan, and an adopted child of her deceased sister) to live upriver with her father in Liwa Raya, the family hunting and agricultural camp along the Río Plátano. When she returned to the coast, Enemecia and her brood stayed at Kuka Denecela's house. Of all the daughters, Enemecia maintained the closest relationship with her mother, Kuka Denecela.

Kuka Denecela's sleeping house and cookhouse were set back in the village, a hundred yards or so from the beach. All of the daughters' homes were close to the kuka's and overlooked an open freshwater well in her patio. The well functioned as the central social station, where the sisters and their daughters washed clothes,

FIGURE 1. Kuka Denecela's sleeping house and cookhouse (PHOTO CREDIT: Peter Herlihy)

FIGURE 2.
Kuka Denecela with pipe (PHOTO CREDIT: Laura Herlihy)

bathed, and held court much of the day. During the days that followed, I watched the sisters attend to their daily domestic activities—cleaning their houses and patios, cooking, caring for the young, and working together in their yucca fields close to the beach. The women visited each other's houses continuously throughout the day. I began to see the tightly knit social and economic networks that existed between the women and how all of the households functioned as part of the larger domestic unit of the matrilocal compound. Then the most obvious question struck me, Where were all the men?

As days turned into weeks I came to know the sisters and other women in Kuri well enough to ask them about their husbands. Most of the men worked as buzos (lobster divers) on boats fishing in Honduran and other international waters; others were upriver hunting and working in their family's agricultural fields along the Río Plátano. Still other men lived in different regions of Moskitia, sharing their time between families, including their other wives and children. It soon became obvious that coastal villages like Kuri were the women and children's domain. The women referred to this phenomenon by their own term, waikna apu, which they used for both permanent and temporary states of being without men.[2]

Figure 3. Children on Kuri's beach
(photo credit: Peter Herlihy)

Strenuous village chores that, following the gendered division of labor in Miskito society, only men could accomplish often presented themselves. In these cases the sisters had to search high and low to find a man. Beneath the heat of the midmorning sun during verano *(the dry season), sisters Delfina, Tomasa, Enemecia, and Ilabia and Neomi, Delfina's cook, had gathered around the natural well in the middle of the kuka's patio, just yards from the opened window of my house. I could see that the activities of the matrigroup had come to a halt. I overheard them talking—the well water had become dirty, which meant that no clothes washing, cooking, cleaning, or bathing could ensue that day. The sisters were lamenting the obvious. They were, as usual, waikna apu.*

A man was needed to descend into the well and dig the shaft deeper, a dirty, hot, time-consuming job. Delfina, who wielded the most power to coerce others, began the manhunt by announcing, "Waikna pliki auna" (I'm off to look for a man). "Kaia maka" (Let's go), she commanded Naomi, her cook. Like soldiers, they walked single file into the monte *(forest), Naomi trailing behind; the two scoured nearby villages for a healthy male body. An hour passed. The women then reappeared with a distant male relative (a former "husband" of a second cousin) who, luckily for them, owed Delfina money. This was quite a find in the city of women, one that reinforced Delfina's ascending status as a kuka and the head of her smaller but blossoming matrigroup.*

Kuka Denecela exited her cookhouse, taking note of the man in the well. She checked under her steps, verifying that her shovel was missing. With her arms folded in front of her, she asked her daughters point blank, "Yang shuvelki ba, yaki briwan bara makabi ai walras kan?" (Who took my shovel without asking?)

Delfina mumbled a profanity under her breath ("hijo de puta" was one of her favorites). The sisters, biting their lips to disguise their laughter, looked away from their mother.

"Hmmm," Kuka snapped her chin upward and released a quick voiced nasal to show that she was insulted. Two short braids flapped at the back of her neck. Glancing at her daughters from the sides of her eyes, rechecking that they were watching her, she yelled defensively, "Yang baman man yaptikam sna, mai wipaia sna" (I'm your mother, it's my job to reprimand you). Kuka marched over, grabbed her shovel, and half pouting, half glaring at her offspring, retreated to her cookhouse.

Entertained that their mother had become uba praut *(self-righteous and brazen), the sisters laughed openly once Kuka was out of earshot. Their nervous laughter acted as a release mechanism for the uncomfortable situation at hand: the sisters had been trying to remain charming, if not flirty, with the man below the ground* so that he would continue cleaning the well. But by chastising the sisters, Kuka had given the impression that their family was tingkikas (unappreciative) of his efforts.

Delfina murmured another ungodly remark. Tomasa, the sister with eight children, giggled uncontrollably and accidently wet her pants. This was noted immediately by her sisters, who reacted with screeches. The energy level remained high, no doubt due to the presence of a strange man in their well. The spirited discourse hinted that it would not be long until Delfina usurped her mother's power. After all, Delfina had stood up to Kuka.

I did not think much less of Delfina for cursing her mother. I reasoned that, after all, it was Delfina who had invested the most time and effort into solving the dirty water problem. In fact, it was the financial debt owed to her that got the man below sea-level in the first place, and after he climbed out of the well, Delfina had her cook prepare a meal for the man, a cost that would not be shared by her mother nor her sisters. As for the man in the well, I had never seen him before that day and I would never see him again.

A Trip up the Río Plátano

Kuri lies in the hub of social and economic activity along the north coast of Moskitia. Connected to ten neighboring coastal villages through a network of footpaths, lagoons, and manmade canals, in addition to the open coastal byway, being on the coast meant being in a relatively cosmopolitan and connected world. Kabura (being on the coast) was being in a social world of visiting friends and families; it was watching the hustle and bustle of people in motion, going to churches, schools, health centers, graveyards, restaurants, and stores. The women in Kuri said they much preferred the coastal ambience over the isolated agricultural camps upriver.

Klaura (being upriver) was a different state of mind than being on the coast. Family agricultural lands with seasonal work camps, called kiamps in Miskitu, champas in Spanish, and camps in English, are situated along the Río Plátano a day or two upriver by pipante (a flat-bottom dugout canoe) and palanca (a pole used to push canoes upriver) from the coastal villages. Being upriver was being in an isolated world, where travel is difficult and one lives close to the elements. Both sun and rain beat down relentlessly on those who traversed the river and worked in the agricultural fields. Upriver was the men's domain.

"The boat is at the landing," Kuka Denecela instructed us as she walked us through the neighborhood of Kusuapaihka to get to the landin (the canal's edge, which villagers used as a natural dock). Three pipantes, constructed for poling

Figure 4. The Evangelical Pentecostal
Church, Kuri, by M. Kendrid, age ten

up and paddling down the rivers, waited at the landing. There were also larger,
barrel-shaped cayucos (round-bottom dugout canoes), built for ocean travel. One
cayuco was painted light blue with an outboard motor attached at the rear. My
guess was correct—this would be ours. Our guide, Alan, a park ranger of sorts
who was married to Enemecia, was already breaking branches in two and shoving
them between the sides of the cayuco for our seats.

The passengers in the pipantes next to ours waited patiently for their boatmen,
wearing plastic bags and towels as hats to protect themselves from the midmorning
sun. Men and women politely said their good-byes along the dock before climbing
aboard their canoes. Shaking hands softly with only the ends of their fingers, they
pressed their faces together and sniffed each other, the customary Miskitu greeting
among friends and family. The locals spoke quietly, saying "aisabe" (good-bye) and
"kaiki was" (be careful), looking down to respectfully avoid eye contact.

"Klaura kaisa?" (Are you going up?), Kuka Denecela asked her friend in one
of the canoes.

"Aouu" (Yes), the woman said, elongating the vowels to make her answer
more emphatic.

Kuka focused in on a young sojourner: "Pain bas" (Behave yourself); she pointed her finger at her grandson Mario in another flat-bottomed canoe. Mario hung his head in shame. "Walram?" (Are you listening?), Kuka threatened him. I later learned that poorly behaved children like Mario were commonly sent upriver as punishment.

Once we were situated in our cayuco, Alan pushed us back a few yards before starting the motor. We continued through the canal, eventually connecting to the Río Plátano some distance from the river's mouth at Barra Plátano (a sandbar that formed where the river empties out to the sea). Heading upriver, we passed two bends of cattle land before we entered Miskitu agricultural and hunting lands. Using one of the few outboard motors then found along the north coast, we passed weighted-down canoes carrying as many as ten people who were headed to their fields. Most were packed with small children and animals—roosters, dogs, and even cats in bags. Other dugouts were filled with produce, heading back down to the coast to sell or share it with family members.

Champas (probably from the English word, camp) stood on high bluffs overlooking the river's edge. These shelters, pole-framed structures with no walls, are

FIGURE 5. A man in a pipante with cargo, Río Plátano (PHOTO CREDIT: Peter Herlihy)

9

reworked yearly for dry season occupancy. From the boat we could see the roofs made of thatched palm and the beds fashioned from bamboo with mosquito netting hooked above them.

By the early afternoon our cayuco reached Liwa Raya, the workplace of Kuka Denecela's matrigroup. The small beach at Liwa Raya had a bench sunken in the sand; a small piece of laundry soap sat on top. We climbed the bluff's slope, each of us carrying our gear, and stopped when we reached the cookhouse. Inside was the fogón, a shelf to store dishes, and a wooden rack above for provisions. Chickens, dogs, and cats scoured the patio for morsels of rice. Children ran behind the small animals to chase them out of the kitchen and patio area.

Behind the open fire stood Enemecia, who was already making coffee for us. Alan hesitated before greeting Enemecia, and then he smiled, bending down to kiss each of the four girls hugging at his legs and waist. Since her separation from Alan, Enemecia had lived in in Liwa Raya and worked the land with her father, Dama (grandfather or respected male elder) Octavio.

Enemecia served us coffee and began preparing dinner. Dama Octavio had hunted that day and killed a tepesquintle (Agouti paca or Cuniculus paca), a large rodent widely sought by the locals for its savory meat. Alan relaxed in the hammock waiting for a home-cooked meal.

It was dark when three men approached the cookhouse. Friends of Octavio, these men somehow had gotten word of Octavio's kill. Alan looked suspiciously at them and then at Enemecia. I helped Enemecia serve and clear the visitors' plates in what seemed like an uncomfortable silence. We poured water over each of their hands from a plastic bowl; afterwards they took the bowl's remaining water, swished it around in their mouths, and spit it out. Next Enemecia and I brought each of them coffee, sugar, and a spoon, waiting while they stirred. This was more domestic work than I had done in months. On the coast we were served our daily meals in Delfina's comedor.

The men disappeared back into the night after finishing their coffee. Alan raked his eyes over Enemecia before inquiring, "Do you have a man up here?" Enemecia scoffed back at him, "Me up here alone with my father and children, and you on the coast drinking and carrying on with your girlfriends, and you have the nerve to ask me that."

At the other end of the patio Octavio opened a bible and handed it to Enemecia's oldest daughter, Rustelia. "Why don't you read to us?" With a group of ten circling around her in hammocks, benches, and chairs, Rustelia read aloud in Spanish. Mario, her twelve-year-old brother (an adopted cousin), was in charge of

Figure 6. Liwa Raya campground
(photo credit: Peter Herlihy)

Figure 7. Cousins eating dinner, Liwa Raya
(photo credit: Peter Herlihy)

keeping slivers of fragrant, slow-burning pine, or leña, *(from the distant savanna)* available for Rustelia to use like a candle.

"Mario," Enemecia bellowed repeatedly as the leña burned out and interrupted the reading.

The men then retired to their hammocks to talk and smoke cigarettes while the children got ready for bed. After Peter had explained his work, Octavio agreed to take Alan and him into the forest the next day. The family woke up at 4:30 a.m., much earlier than people on the coast. By 6:00 a.m. Enemecia and Rustelia had cooked, served, and cleaned up breakfast; the children had hauled water and chopped firewood for the day; and Peter, Alan, and Octavio had left on a ten-plus-mile hunting trip into the pristine, tall forest. Enemecia planned to work her fields, and I would write up field notes on the patio and in hammocks at Liwa Raya.

"Rustelia," Enemecia turned to her daughter and smiled, "Do you want to work today?" Rustelia ran to the house, grabbed her gear, and returned. "Ready," she said with spirit. The mother and daughter looked like warriors with their rubber boots, pants under their dresses, heads wrapped in bandanas to keep insects out, and machetes resting on their shoulders.

"Mario," Enemecia added as an afterthought, "you stay here and watch the children and the patio." Mario's lip quivered and he began to cry silently, turning his head away to hide his tears from the others. Mario was twelve and Rustelia was thirteen. She could still beat him in wrestling.

We left Liwa Raya three days later and headed back downriver to the coast. Enemecia was sullen. We said our good-byes at the small beach. "We'll be back," I said, while giving Enemecia a final hug.

"Oh, yeah," Enemecia quipped, releasing me from her embrace. "You're not gonna come back, you're going to forget about Liwa Raya." Enemecia was responding to me but glaring directly into Alan's eyes.

A canoe moved upriver with a woman and her husband from Utla Almuk, a coastal village to the southeast of Kuri. The woman called to Enemecia, "Your sister Tomasa said she can't come up this week . . . the baby's still sick. She said that she'll come next week." The woman nodded to indicate the end of the message. She used her whole body's strength to push her palanca into the river bottom and propel the pipante onward against the current.

"Oh, yeah?" Enemecia asked rhetorically. "When will Tomasa ever come?" Enemecia's remark betrayed the antagonism she felt toward her more social, coastal-dwelling sisters. She thought her sisters made excuses not to come upriver.

"*The fields are cleaned, and still they don't come to plant . . . they've already been cleaned,*" she repeated, to emphasize that she and Octavio had completed the most arduous part of the work.

Alan shoved us off from the beach. I stood in our canoe examining Enemecia. I realized that she had acquired a hardened state of mind. A single mother living off the land in the monte, Enemecia provided her children with vegetables, grains, meat, and fish in a respectable way. She had even begun to hunt with her father. Like her mother, Kuka Denecela, Enemecia thought it disgraceful to earn money the way her sisters did on the coast. In Enemecia's opinion, her sisters had sold out by turning their homes into bodegas for the lobster divers.

Meat, Men, and Money

During the lobster-diving off-season, or veda, Miskitu men return to shore for three to four months. The veda occurs at a fortuitous time in the yearly agricultural calendar, when men travel upriver to complete the labor-intensive work of harvesting crops, clearing fields, and replanting. Women remaining in the coastal villages are left without money and little access to food. Toward the end of the 1997 lobster-diving off-season, Kuka Denecela and her daughters looked defeated. After weeks of eating nothing but beans, rice, and bananas, their world was monotonous, their outlook on life, bleak. One particularly still afternoon Kuka sat on her steps and lamented to me, "*Huina apu, waikna apu, lalah apu, pruamna*" (No meat, no men, no money, I'm gonna die).

Curious, I asked, "*Ani kao brin mai daukisa?*" (Which of the three—meat, men, or money—do you want the most?).

"*Huina*" (Meat), she answered with no hesitation. "*Windarku kais. Waikna kum luaia sa. Ai pakitka lalah bri ba kuna ahkia kaikramki huina pis kum balsi wan?*" (Look out the window. You're bound to see a man pass by, sure to have money in his pocket, but when's the last time you've seen a piece of meat walk by?) Accessing a man and, subsequently, his money was merely a means to an end for her. Meat was a highly valued and increasingly scarce resource in coastal villages. Once hunted regularly and shared between related families, meat was now mainly purchased with cash from stores and spontaneous markets consisting of the slaughtered animal, a scale, a butcher knife, and a table.

Without money to buy meat, women like Kuka remained depressed for the entire off-season. But women returned to their more high-spirited selves with the *opening of the lobster-diving season that August. Excitement prevailed as the lobster boats, merchandise boats, and advance payments to the divers all arrived together and answered their prayers.*

Kuka and her daughters Delfina and Tomasa sat on the beach, looking out to the sea to witness the first boats reaching the coast. Delfina raised her nose to the wind and said, "Lalah kia waowisa" (The smell of money is in the air). The women's hunger for meat crested as each wave broke across the shoreline. Tomasa rubbed her hands together in anticipation: "Ini minit" (Any minute now). The women were not waiting helplessly, dependent merely on the kindness and generosity of the men. They already had stacked the cards in their favor by concocting and using magic potions to help them manipulate the male divers into giving them their wages.

BOOK SUMMARY

The Mermaid and the Lobster Diver is an ethnographic journey into the everyday lives of indigenous Miskitu women and men in northeastern Honduras. The book builds on the works of anthropologists Mary Helms and Philip Dennis, who both completed their field research in Nicaragua. Helms (1971) portrays the Miskitu people in Asang, a community along the middle Río Coco, just after the bust in the pine-lumbering industry. Dennis (2004) describes Awastara, a coastal Miskitu community near Cape Gracias a Dios where men participated in the green-sea-turtle industry and had access to other wage-earning jobs. My book gives a picture of Kuri (pop. 175), a third community in a different part of the Miskitu world, on the north coast of Honduras in the Río Plátano Biosphere Reserve, with a different sort of economic base—the deepwater lobster-diving industry.

The book explores Plátano Miskitu social organization at the height of the lobster-diving economy. Kuri's social organization in the late 1990s was profoundly female centered. Astoundingly, 90 percent of the households in 1991, and 84 percent in 1988, were female headed. These households tied into matrilocal groups where senior women (kukas) held positions of authority within the family and descent was increasingly traced through the female line. Male absenteeism also existed within the north coast villages of the Plátano biosphere. Plátano Miskitu men lived away from their families during the lobster-diving season (August–March). The men worked on boats for twelve days at a time and returned home for only a few days between trips. During the lobster-diving veda, or off-season (April–July), the men lived upriver in agricultural and hunting camps located at some distance from the coastal village. This contribution to the ethnographic literature presents a much more female-centered society than has previously been documented for the Miskitu people.

Differences in life strategies exist between women in the western world and women in the Honduran Moskitia. Miskitu women do not want equal work opportunities but instead put their energies into becoming mothers and heads of households and accessing cash salaries of men. Girls begin an apprenticeship in mothering at a young age (eight to ten years old), when they are given full responsibility for taking care of a small child. Young women usually give birth to their own child when they are around eighteen or nineteen. For teenage girls, motherhood functions as a rite of passage to womanhood, as new mothers soon become the head of a household and are incorporated into the social and economic reciprocity networks of the matrigroup. Sisters raise their children together as part of one large family and work in coalitions to gain access to the divers' earnings.

Sexual magic (*praidi saihka*) is one of the most successful and broadly used strategies that women employ to gain access to the men's earnings. Miskitu women utilize sexual magic as a tool to keep men attached to them and to ensure that men continue providing them with money. My research describes for the first time in the ethnographic literature that Miskitu women use praidi saihka for economic survival. The research also demonstrates that Miskitu men and women engage in transactional sexual relations where women are given a gift of cash (*mairin mana*) in exchange for sex. Coastal Miskitu people do not consider this practice an act of prostitution, mainly because the women who receive the money are often in love and in a relationship with the diver. Miskitu women, then, are reinventing their healing and sexual practices within the context of the expanding market economy.

Consumerism plays a central role in coastal life for women and men—fetishism for cash and for store-bought goods rules the day. Plátano women appear emotionally fulfilled when in the act of purchasing food and goods at stores, an act that they complete some three times a day. When lobster divers are paid cash back on shore, they go on spending sprees at the more than a hundred small stores that line the seven-kilometer coastal byway. Men drinking beer and rum (*guaro*) at the stores and walking between villages are easy targets for rapacious women. The fact that men have money that women desire pits men and women against each other, and their relationships have a resoundingly commodified edge. Women view men as commodities and even call them *lalah dusa* (money bags). The pathos of male-female relationships appears especially in true-to-life and moving situations that I describe using short stories and song and incantation lyrics, which are interspersed throughout the book.

About 90 percent of the Miskitu boys and men along the north coast of the Plátano biosphere have worked as deepwater divers in the binational (Honduras–United States) lobster industry. Divers earned about $4,800 (U.S.) per year in the late 1990s, inflated wages for the region and significantly above the average national income. Although lobster diving is lucrative, it is also a life-threatening occupation—about 15 percent of the divers (around a hundred men) have been injured or killed on the job, mainly due to decompression sickness, or the bends. Divers continue diving because they feel they have no other choice, as diving is the only cash-earning job available to them at a time when the global market economy is rapidly expanding.

Decompression sickness is referred to locally as *liwa mairin siknis* (Mermaid sickness). Within Miskitu folklore and mythology, the Mermaid is the main Miskitu water spirit, owner of all fresh- and saltwater resources. Miskitu men, women, and children tell stories of how the Mermaid punishes divers with sickness and death for extracting too many of her lobsters. Yet, at the same time, manhood in Miskitu society is partially hinged upon the men's ability to catch lobsters and provide money to women. Men constantly battle the dual pressures of fulfilling the women's desire for cash and staying healthy. Men live anxious lives, fearing not only the wrath of the supernatural *liwa mairin* but also the wrath of everyday women who use magic potions to control men's sexuality and wages. Miskitu women's agency, then, is manifested in both goddess and human form.

I invoke the images of the Mermaid and the lobster diver for the title of the book because they are archetypes of femininity and masculinity on the Miskito Coast. The Mermaid, known for being a money-hungry femme fatale, uses her supernatural sexuality to control and, ultimately, to bring harm to men. The lobster diver, viewed as a brave and generous man, risks his life in a dangerous occupation to provide gifts of cash to women. The perceived interactions between the Mermaid and the lobster diver not only demonstrate the commodification of gendered selves in Miskitu society but also underscore the power associated with women's sexuality and the vulnerable position of men.

PART I

Historical Fact and Anthropological Fiction

CHAPTER ONE

The Miskito Coast

History, Place, Identity

THE MÍSKÍTO COAST (NORTHEASTERN HONDURAS AND NÍCARAGUA) is the binational homeland of the indigenous Miskitu people.

Miskitu people trace their ancestry to the mid-seventeenth century, when Misumalpan, Macro-Chibchan-speaking Amerindian women residing at Cape Gracias a Dios married British and other Europeans, mulattos, and black free men and slaves. In 1710, ethnohistorian Mary W. Helms reports, nine hundred blacks were brought to the Miskito Coast from Ghana, Gambia, Togo, and Benin. The black men married Indian women, who then raised their mixed-race children as culturally Miskitu (Helms 1971:23–28; Newson 1986:283). Helms (1971) and Eduard Conzemius (1932) contend that intermarriage continued from the seventeenth through the nineteenth century. Helms (1976:9) says of the Miskitu: "These so-called Indians are a biologically mixed people originating during the colonial period from miscegenation between indigenous women of eastern Nicaragua and British settlers, buccaneers, and especially Negro freemen and slaves who sought the isolated shore as refugees from Spanish and West Indian colonies or were brought to the coast as laborers by English planters."

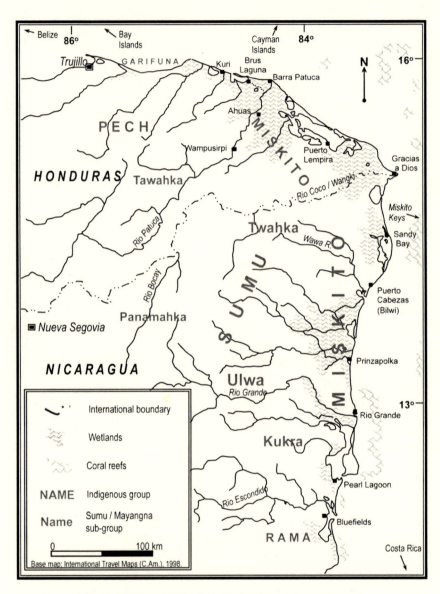

MAP 4. The Miskito Coast (Map Credit: Kendra McSweeney, 2011)

Due to their mixed-race identity (black and Indian), the colonial Miskitu became known as Zambos y Mosquitos, Zambos-Mosquitos, or just Zambos.[1] The Zambos-Mosquitos expanded as a population group during the colonial era, while most other Amerindian populations diminished in numbers and experienced significant culture and language loss. Helms (1977:158–59) reports that the success of the colonial Miskitu people was due to their positive interactions with outside economies (see also Holm 1978:186). Most significantly, they expanded their territory and refortified their ethnic identity through interactions with the British. The British made political and economic alliances with the Miskitu, armed them with muskets, and hired the men to fight against the Spanish. Miskitu militiamen also raised their muskets to dominate the neighboring Pech (commonly called Paya) and Tawahka-Sumu (who speak one of the Misumalpan languages) indigenous groups through a "raiding and trading" economy. Some scholars have theorized that the name of the Miskitu people came from the word "musket," yet geographer Bill Davidson (personal communication, Honduras, 1997) contends that the people were named for the Mosquito Keys, a group of small islands located just off the coast of Cape Gracias a Dios.

THE BRITISH PRESENCE

The British originally colonized the Central American Caribbean lowlands mainly because the Spanish Crown had rejected the idea, due to the region's small population numbers and the lack of gold, silver, and other precious metals. By the mid-seventeenth century the British more broadly established their presence in the Greater Antilles along the Miskito Coast, in the islands off the Nicaraguan coast, and in Jamaica, Grand Cayman, and later, Belize. Jamaica became the seat of the British Crown and Grand Cayman, its military outpost. Belize was declared a formal British colony and the Miskito Coast, a British protectorate. The trading triangle developed between Jamaica, Belize, and the Miskito Coast, mainly for the British to extract logwoods such as mahogany for shipment to England (Naylor 1989; Parsons 1954).

The British employed their colonial policy of indirect rule over the Miskito Coast from 1650 to 1786, creating a colonial political system modeled after their own and even designating a native "King of Mosquitia" (Helms 1971:20).[2] The British influence was greatest from 1730, with the founding of Black River (and also Cape Gracias and Bluefields), to the Anglo-Spanish Convention in 1786. Black River, called Palacios today, served as the main British agricultural colony, the largest fortified settlement, and the administrative center (capital seat) of the Central American Caribbean coast. Black River was home to British settlers who built sugarcane, cotton, and cacao plantations, cut mahogany, kept livestock, owned slaves, and traded with the Pech, Tawahka, Zambos-Mosquitos, and, illicitly, with the interior Spanish (Hale 1987b:33–57; Naylor 1989:39–45).

The Spanish unsuccessfully attempted to remove the British from the shore in 1763 with the Treaty of Paris and in 1783 with the related Treaty of Versailles. Finally, in 1786, the Anglo-Spanish Convention forced the British to pull out of Black River; however, they retained informal or de facto power over the region (Floyd 1967:169; Pim and Seemann 1869:312). The Spanish could not attract settlers to Black River, mainly due to the presence of the Zambos-Mosquitos, who were known for being hostile toward the Spanish (Gonzalez 1988:53; Laird 1970:9; Newson 1986:257). The Zambos-Mosquitos' friendly relations with the British and hatred of the Spanish defined their interethnic relations during the colonial era (Hale 1994).

The Miskito Coast maintained its status as a British protectorate even after Central American independence in 1823. However, the region was reincorporated into the Honduran republic in the early 1860s. North American businessmen entered the region about the same time and began hiring Honduran Miskitu men to exploit logwood, fruit and rubber trees, and other local resources. English-speaking German Moravian missionaries asserted their presence in Honduran Moskitia in the early twentieth century. The British North American businessmen and the Moravians left an indelible imprint on the region, and English is still the prestige language spoken along the coast (Hale 1987b, 1994; Helms 1971; Conzemius 1932).

The Miskitu people lost their social and economic dominance on the coast after the British abolished the slave trade in 1807 (and slavery in 1833–1835). By the 1820s Creoles and Black Caribs (Garífuna) had filled most positions on the plantations and had replaced the Miskitu as the major wage-earning populations on the shore (Gonzalez 1988:55–56; Hale 1987b:33–43). Helms (1977) points out that the Creoles and the Black Caribs also replaced the Zambos-Mosquitos as the most Negroid or black group on the coast. The presence of the Creoles and the Black Caribs, combined with the fact that Miskitu people began marrying Pech and Tawahka "Indians," resulted in both the Honduran and Nicaraguan states referring to them as the "Miskitu Indians" in all legal documents by the mid-nineteenth century. The Miskitu continued to be identified as Indians throughout the twentieth century, until they became recognized internationally as "indigenous" (Helms 1977:162–65).[3] Helms (1977) believes that because of the changing constellations of populations on the coast, the Miskitu switched their identity from Indian to black and then back again to Indian over the past four hundred years. The Miskitu people's shifting identity through time and across space is an important part of their complex history.

SETTLEMENT HISTORY OF THE NORTH COAST VILLAGES

In the early 1800s Mosquito-Zambo General Robinson lived in an English-style house at Río Plátano. Robinson owned Indian and black slaves, kept cattle, and traded sarsaparilla with the interior Pech (Offen 1999). Robinson also controlled the coastal region between the Ríos Tinto and Patuca, including the settlements of the newly arrived Garífuna people near the mouth of the Río Patuca—Garífuna families settled in Barra Patuca in 1804 but retreated shortly after to the Black River area. A smallpox epidemic in the 1840s reduced the coastal Honduran Miskitu population, and by 1860, when Moskitia was reincorporated into the Honduran state, only five or six Miskitu hamlets were settled between Río Tinto (the Black River) and Río Plátano (Herlihy and Herlihy 1991).

The United Fruit Company (UFC) worked on the Ríos Plátano and Paulaya-Sico and in the mountainous Baltimore region by the early 1900s. UFC had a major economic impact on the region, hiring Miskitu and other indigenous, black, and European men to work as wage laborers, supervisors, and company heads. Alton Bruner, a North American director for UFC, had his *cocal* (coconut plantation) in Cocobila and opened the region's first store in Jaloba ("haul over" in English), a neighborhood near Plaplaya, where La Criba meets the Río Paulaya. The Miskitu, Pech, Tawahka, and others traveled great distances to acquire western goods from Bruner's store, thus creating a culturally plural social milieu in the economic hub of the region.

Miskitu people in the early twentieth century expanded along the coast and established the settlements of Barra Plátano, Cocobila, and Ibans (see map 2). By the 1920s new Miskitu hamlets had developed in Utla Almuk and Kuri and Europeans had settled to the east in Payabila and Platubila. Cocobila and Barra Plátano grew larger, each acquiring stores, a school, and a Moravian church. The Moravian Reverend George Heath, who lived in Cocobila, walked along the beach path to Barra Plátano to give Sunday service.

In 1947 some Miskitu residents left an overcrowded Cocobila to clear monte to the east, forming Belén (now 59 households and 353 individuals); and in 1982 others settled New Jerusalem (today with 73 households and 438 individuals). New Jerusalem's Buenos Aires neighborhood has grown and now reaches the easternmost houses of Belén. Cocobila was originally the most developed community on the coastal strip; however, Belén now has more communication and transportation networks connecting it the outside world, including an airfield (established in 1981) for small planes to land.

The Río Plátano Biosphere Reserve

UNESCO's Man and the Biosphere (UN-MAB) program established the Río Plátano Biosphere Reserve in 1980 to protect the natural and cultural resources of the region.[4]

The Plátano biosphere encompasses over eight thousand kilometers of spectacular rainforest, coastal, and lagoon habitats and includes three indigenous groups (Miskitu, Pech, and Garífuna) that total about twenty thousand

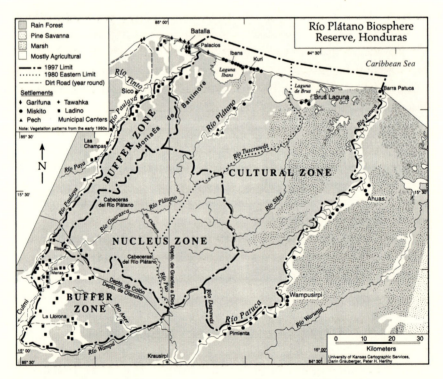

MAP 2. Río Plátano Biosphere Reserve (Map Credit: Peter Herlihy, 2001)

individuals, over twenty thousand Ladino (Spanish-speaking mestizo) colonists, and the English-speaking Creoles and Isleños. Adding to the ethnic diversity, the indigenous Tawahka people reside along the middle Río Patuca, just outside the Plátano biosphere's southeastern boundary.

The Miskitu people (pop. 17,874) are the largest, most expansive indigenous population in the Plátano biosphere, with settlements and agricultural and hunting lands along the north coast and along the Ríos Patuca, Plátano, and Tinto-Paulaya. While Barra Patuca (pop. 2,237) and Brus Lakun (pop. 1,811) are the largest Miskitu communities, several small towns have populations of around a thousand. Most Miskitu settlements are really small villages of around two hundred individuals. (P. Herlihy 1993:54–62; 2001:101–2).

The Miskitu, the Pech, the Garífuna, and Ladinos have historically inhabited different regions, separated by cultural buffer zones. Today, however, they live in a complex distribution pattern with overlapping areas of settlement and resource exploitation. In the northern zone the Miskitu intermarry and live in mixed villages with the indigenous Pech and Garífuna and Central American English-speaking Creoles and Isleños. Just beyond the southern limits of the reserve they also intermarry and live in mixed villages with the indigenous Tawahka. Many groups have assimilated the dominant Miskitu cultural practices and now speak their language. While it remains true that the Miskitu, for the most part, dominate the Pech, the Tawahka, Creoles, and Isleños within and just beyond the biosphere, they do not exert the same influence over their Garífuna and Ladino neighbors, who both resist being assimilated and dominated by the Miskitu (Herlihy and Herlihy 1991:9–15).

Spanish functions as the reserve's lingua franca because of its stature as the national language and because it is taught in all elementary schools. In the biosphere's southern zone the large population of Spanish-speaking mestizo colonists (called "Ladinos" or "Indios" locally) has heightened hegemonic influence stemming from Honduras's national culture and modernization. Yet in the northern zone Miskitu is the most widely spoken indigenous language. Pech is the most threatened language today due to assimilation to Miskitu language and culture.

Honduran Miskitu Racial Identity

The political and ethnic identity of the Nicaraguan Miskitu population (pop. 145,000) has been well-covered in the social scientific literature, while considerably less research has focused on the smaller Honduran population (pop. 35,000). This literature has represented the modern-day Nicaragua Miskitu people as "Indians" within the Latin American nation-state, politicizing their identity as guerilla fighters in the Sandinista revolution (1979–1990) and the U.S.-backed Contra war (1984–1987) (Richard Adams 1981; Bourgois 1981; Dennis 1981; Diskin 1991; Falla 1982; Hale 1987a, 1987b, 1994; Nietschmann 1989; Vilas 1989). When speaking in their native Miskitu language, Nicaraguan Miskitu people do refer to themselves as "Indiyin," and those who speak Creole English also call themselves "Indian." In contrast to this, my research found that Honduran Miskitu speakers perceive themselves to be more racially "mixed" than their Nicaraguan kinsmen. I remember the day I asked Enemecia, a Miskitu woman from Kuri, if she considered herself to be an "Indiyin." Enemecia replied, "Indiyin . . . ba dia. Yang nani Indiyin nani apia sna. Yang nani sika sambo, mestizo, bara mulato. Yawan alsut sika mikst . . . Yawan sika Miskitu ba Miskitu aisisa ba mita" (Indians? We are not Indians. . . . We are Zambos, mestizos, and mulattos, we are all mixed. . . . We are Miskitu because we speak Miskitu.).

FIGURE 8. A Ladino family along the Río Paulaya
(PHOTO CREDIT: Peter Herlihy)

This research illustrates that at the time of my fieldwork in the late 1990s Honduran Miskitu speakers did not refer to or socio-racially classify themselves as "Indiyin," nor did they refer to themselves as "Indios" when speaking Spanish (very few Honduran Miskitu individuals speak Creole English). I collected the ethnic labels that Miskitu speakers used when communicating in their own language as well as the terms they utilized when speaking Spanish. The terms reveal the socio-racial categories Miskitu individuals ascribed to themselves and others. I also documented the broad spectrum of ethnic terms that groups use and receive in the Plátano biosphere. Most significantly, I documented that the Afro-indigenous Garífuna, the indigenous Miskitu and Pech, the Central American English-speaking Creoles and Isleños, and even the Spanish-speaking Ladinos (mestizos) themselves refer to the Ladinos as "Indios" (Indians) when speaking in Spanish (see tables 1 and 2). This reveals one of the several compelling cases of identity inversion on the north coast (L. Herlihy 2002, 2008).

TABLE 1. Broad spectrum of ethnic labels

	RECIPIENT					
REFERENT	Miskitu	Pech	Garífuna	Ladino	Creole	Isleño
Miskitu	Miskitu	Paya	Karibi	Ispael	Kriul	Musti
Pech	Kumaja	Pech	Karabe	Bula	Tersu	Turucawa
Garífuna	Idudu	Fayana	Garífuna	Muladu	Guio	Wadabu
Ladino	Zambo	Paya	Moreno	Ladino/Indio	Negro	Caracol
Creole	Miskito	Paya	Carib	Spanish	Creole	English
Isleño	Miskito	Paya	Carib	Spanish	Creole	English

Source: L. Herlihy 2008:132.

TABLE 2. Polite and derogatory Spanish terms of reference

HIGH/POLITE	LOW/DEROGATORY
Miskitu	Zambo
Pech	Paya
Garífuna	Moreno/Negro
Ladino	Indio
Ingles Negro	Negro
Isleño	Caracol

Source: L. Herlihy 2008:133.

FIGURE 9.
An Isleño man in Utla Almuk
(PHOTO CREDIT: Laura Herlihy)

The Honduran Miskitu do, however, refer to their neighboring Nicaraguan Miskitu kin as "Indiyin." Interviews with Kuri residents revealed that Honduran Miskitu people perceive their Nicaraguan kinsmen to be more "Indian" than themselves. Many Kuri residents commented to me that the Nicaraguan Miskitu people were more "pure," more like their "original" Amerindian ancestors.[5] This may be a lingering feature of historic consequences. Linda Newson (1986:22) contends that the Nicaraguan Miskitu became Indians earlier than the Honduran Miskitu, who were thought of as a mixed "Negroid" group up until Central American Independence in 1823: "As a mixed racial group the Zambos-Mosquitos as a whole cannot be classified as Indians any more than mestizos, and this is particularly true for the Honduran sector of the Shore, where the negro influence was strongest. As such, the Zambos-Miskitos are not regarded as Indians at the end of the colonial period."

Karl Offen (1999, 2002) contends that the Miskitu people were divided into separate ethnic groups during the colonial era: the more pure "Indians" (the Tawira) lived in Nicaragua, while the group that was more mixed with blacks, known as Zambos-Moskitos, lived near Black River. My scholarship

HISTORICAL FACT AND ANTHROPOLOGICAL FICTION

argues that the present-day Honduran Miskitu continue to make up a separate culture group, distinct from the Nicaraguan Miskitu Indians, and contribute to the emerging mixed-race identity of the Honduran Miskitu people (L. Herlihy 2002, 2008; see also Pérez Chiriboga 2002).

Construction of Indianness

Río Plátano Miskitu people perceive themselves to be similar to the Tawahka and Pech peoples, who were autochthonous Amerindians before contact. One Miskitu elder told me, "We are all descendants from rain-forest tribes [*tribus de la selva*]." My interviews with Plátano Miskitu individuals, however, reveal that they see themselves as being more advanced than their Tawahka and Pech neighbors. Pech individuals are especially stereotyped as ignorant, docile farmers and hunters. Río Plátano elementary students have a yearly contest known as Indio Lempira, where students dress as "Indians" and the winner is invariably a Pech child from the Las Marías region. The Miskitu perceive the level of Indianness in Honduran Moskitia as a range, from least to most.

Levels of Indianness:
    Miskitu → Tawahka → Pech

FIGURE 10. A Miskitu family
(PHOTO CREDIT: Peter Herlihy)

Figure 11. A Tawahka family in Krausirpe
(PHOTO CREDIT: Peter Herlihy)

Figure 12. Pech women in Las Marías
(PHOTO CREDIT: Vince Murphy)

Construction of Blackness

When speaking informally in Spanish, the groups with African ancestry—the Miskitu, Creoles, and the Garífuna—all use the terms "Zambo" (to refer to the Miskitu), "Negro" (to refer to the Creoles), and "Moreno" (to refer to the Garífuna) to invoke each other's African ancestry (table 1). The perceived level of blackness from the Miskitu perspective also ranges, from least to most (L. Herlihy 2008).

Level of blackness:
    Miskitu → Creole → Garífuna

Skin color is the most important criteria for blackness, a construct that is based also on hair, face, and body type; cultural and linguistic characteristics; and sexuality.

FIGURE 13.
Creole women from Payabila (PHOTO CREDIT: Laura Herlihy)

FIGURE 14. Garífuna women in Plaplaya
(PHOTO CREDIT: Peter Herlihy)

In my interviews, the Miskitu claimed that European traits constitute standards of beauty, whereas African traits represent the reverse. Within Miskitu communities, many women and men openly commented that their lighter-skinned children were better looking than their darker-skinned children (see also Bonner 1999; Lancaster 1991; Wright 1995). Ugliness was normally associated with blackness. Indeed, darker-skinned people are teased as being *karibi* (Garífuna-like), *uba siksa* (too black), and therefore *saura* (ugly). These perceptions also have been found on the Nicaraguan Atlantic coast, where Miskitu and Creole women with dark skin and physical features associated with blackness have low self-esteem (Antonio et al. 2006).

Plátano Miskitu men and women reproduce colonial stereotypes of the dangerous and sexualized black male (see Anderson 2001; Chevannes 2001). The following song, "Tuktan mairin painkira" (Young beautiful girl), mentions the sexual reputation of men from four different ethnic groups—Miskitu, Ispael (Ladino), Kriul (Creole), and Nikru or Karibi (Garífuna). The song is narrated from the perspective of a Miskitu man whose girlfriend abandoned him and had sexual relations with other men to acquire resources and money, resources that she originally asked him for. The song depicts Creole and Garífuna men,

HISTORICAL FACT AND ANTHROPOLOGICAL FICTION

representing the two groups most associated with blackness, as the most sexually threatening and dangerous men.

Tuktan mairin painkira	Young beautiful girl
Tuktan mairin painkira	Young beautiful girl
sop kum na briwasi	you asked me to bring you to a shop
platuki na briwasi	you asked me to bring you plantains
kraunki nara briwasi	you asked me to bring you a crown
tuktan mairin painkira	young beautiful girl
Miskitu boi kum wiki	then a Miskitu guy arrived
kiamamra kangban kan	he punished you
ai swira lukata	you had tossed away your shame
tuktan mairin painkira	young beautiful girl
Ispael boi kum wiki	then a Ladino guy arrived
platka tara kaiki kan	having seen all of his big money
platu saura brisi aikbia	a little penis he will give to you
tutan mairin painkira	young beautiful girl
tisku mapa tawikan	in a little while it turned out
Kriul boi kum wiki	then a Creole guy arrived
kiamamra kangban kan	he punished you
ai swira lukata	you had thrown away your shame
Kriul mita tawiki	the Creole came back
kaisa bara cuartora	let's go to your room
cuartora briwa ka	when he took you to the room
tuktan mairin painkira	oh beautiful girl
Nikru traus daiki kan	the Garífuna took off his pants
Nikru prak daiki kan	the Garífuna took off his shirt
tuktan mairin sibrikan	the young girl was scared
tuktan mairin sip apia	the young girl couldn't
tisku mapa tawikan	a little later it turned out
Nikru maka dusara	the Garífuna got a big erection like a tree
pabula ba na kangbi kan	he was touching the top of the mosquito netting
ai Nikru dan pruna	oh Garífuna, you're killing me

tuktan mairin sip apia	the young girl couldn't take it
tuktan mairin ini kan	the young girl was crying
ai nikru dan pruna	oh Garífuna man, you're killing me
tawa tawa ai taibram	slowly and forcefully he mounted me
Nikru maka playara	the Garífuna was already in my uterus
ark ini kan	the girl was screaming and crying
ai Nikru dan pruna	oh Garífuna, I'm dying
tawa tawa ai taibram	slowly and forcefully he mounted me

Narrated from the perspective of a Miskitu speaker, the song refers to the Garífuna man as "Nikru" (Negro), a derogatory name used for a Garífuna person. This condescending attitude may reflect historic ethnic conflicts between the Miskitu and Garífuna. The Miskitu and Garífuna were pitted against each other during the colonial period, and they allied with the English and Spanish, respectively. Another factor that made them competitors in the early twentieth century was that the Garífuna gained more social and economic benefits than the Miskitu from their involvement with the banana industry. Nancie Gonzalez (1988) and Mark Anderson (1997) claim that the Miskitu resented the successes of the Garífuna on banana plantations. This may affect Miskitu-Garífuna interactions today in the Plátano biosphere. When the two groups interact socially, they commonly accuse each other of "witchcraft." In the northwestern corner of the Plátano biosphere, Miskitu and Garífuna settlement patterns overlap around Black River, or La Criba, with the Garífuna to the north and the Miskitu to the south (Davidson 1976; P. Herlihy 2001). Conflicts over land rights have ensued between the Miskitu and Garífuna. Sharleen Mollett (2006) describes how the Garífuna are learning to articulate their identity as indigenous people in order to claim ancestral rights to territory (see also Brondo 2010).

Situational Identity
Colonial ideologies of race persist today along the coast. Miskitu individuals still invoke a bond between *meriki* (gringo or North American) people and themselves based on their common past—a historic alliance with the British (Hale 1994). At the same time, Miskitu-speakers try to distance themselves from both blackness and Indianness by reproducing anti-black and anti-Indian ideologies. Most blatantly, the Plátano Miskitu use recursive markers such as skin color, sexual behavior, and ancestry to authenticate and distance

themselves from the ethnic antipodes of blackness and Indianness. Analysis suggests that a dual system of racism persists along the Honduran Caribbean coast, a borderland region where both Latin American and Caribbean ideologies of "race" collide (Wade 1997; Yelvington 2001).

Despite the fact that the indigenous Miskitu people experience racism at the international and national levels and are called Zambos by Spanish speakers, they themselves promulgate racist stereotypes. Plátano Miskitu men and women, then, reinforce the hegemonic, nationalist discourse on socio-racial identities, a discourse that keeps blacks, Indians, and mixed groups like themselves at the bottom of the social hierarchy. My research reveals the deep-rooted and indelible imprint of colonialism and early twentieth century U.S. racist ideologies along the Miskito Coast.

The degree to which Miskitu individuals, as members of a mixed group living in a pluri-ethnic region, see themselves as either black or Indian is related to the group with whom they are interacting. Plátano Miskitu consider themselves more Indian when interacting with the Afro-Caribbean Creole and Afro-indigenous Garífuna peoples but more black when interacting with the indigenous Pech and Tawahka. Plátano Miskitu identity, then, is highly relational (L. Herlihy 2002). Miskitu individuals create "situational identities" in which the self is formed during social interactions with others (Mead 1964). Living in a pluri-ethnic region provides situations where the Miskitu self can take on several different social identities.

More recent interactions between Honduran and Miskitu political leaders and townspeople have influenced Honduran Miskitu people's view of their race and ethnicity. During my return trip to the north coast in 2010, I heard for the first time Honduran Miskitu speakers calling themselves "Insin" or "Indiyin" in their native Miskitu language. Lobster divers I interviewed claimed that this change has resulted from their interactions with Jamaicans, who refer to the Miskitu as "Indian men" in everyday speech. Additionally, a festival that began in 2007 called Sihkru Tara first brought Honduran and Nicaraguan Miskitu peoples together in a show of their common ethnicity and binational homeland. The main Miskitu political party and indigenous movement, Yatama, initiated Sihkru Tara as a festival celebrating Miskitu dance, music, and culture to take place in Nicaragua and Honduras in alternating years. Sihkru Tara activities coincide with the UN-developed International Day of the World's Indigenous People, celebrated each year on August 9. During Sihkru Tara, Nicaraguan Miskitu leaders promote a binational Miskitu indigenous identity and refer to themselves together as "Indiyin" in formal speeches.[6] In an effort to copy Nicaraguan Miskitu leaders, who are perceived as being more politically advanced, Honduran Miskitu political leaders have also adopted the word "Indiyin" (from the Nicaraguan Wangki Miskitu dialect). Despite these more recent changes in Honduran Miskitu perceptions of their racial and ethnic identity, my research demonstrates that they did not view themselves as "Indians" at the close of the twentieth century.

THE RÍO PLÁTANO MISKITU PEOPLE

The "Río Plátano Miskitu" refers to the Miskitu families who live between New Jerusalem and Barra Plátano (east to west, see map 2). These families share agricultural and hunting lands up the Río Plátano. Kuri is tied most closely to the three beachfront villages directly to its east—Tasbapauni, Platubila (really, a hamlet), and Utla Almuk. These villages are connected to each other by the beach, a footpath, and a manmade canal system. The canal, a network of narrow canals and lagoons, extends from the eastern edge of Ibans Lagoon to the

FIGURE 15. The mouth of the Río Plátano
(PHOTO CREDIT: Peter Herlihy)

Río Plátano.[7] Prior to the digging of the canal in the early 1980s, canoe traffic from the river only reached Tasbapauni, and Kuri residents had to walk overland from there to haul their river produce to their homes.

During the rainy season (from June to December), the Tampa Tingni Lagoon cuts an outlet to the sea and Kuri, Utla Almuk, Platubila, and Tasbapauni are left on an island bounded by the lagoon to Kuri's west, Río Plátano to the east, the Caribbean sea to the north, and the canal to the south. To reach the seasonal island, locals cross Tampa Tingni Lagoon or the Río Plátano by water "taxi," paying one or two *lempiras* (the national currency; two lempiras are about fifteen cents) to cross in a canoe.[8] Residents of these villages are linked together not only by transportation and communication networks but also through kinship networks. Children roam freely between villages and a family atmosphere prevails.

CHAPTER TWO

Gendered
Ethnography in Kuri

MY BOOK BUILDS UPON MARY HELMS'S (1971) NOW-CLASSIC
ethnography *Asang: Adaptations to Culture Contact in a Miskito Community*.
Helms recognizes that Miskitu men have worked for North American and
other international companies in various boom and bust extractive economies
since the mid-nineteenth century. The cycle begins with a boom phase, when
Miskitu men earn wages working for foreign companies, which is then followed
by a bust stage as companies overexploit a local resource and then leave the
region. Helms argues that Miskitu social organization varied according to the
phase of the boom and bust economic model in which they were participating.
She states that during boom phases men became migrant wage-laborers and
women bonded together in matrilocal groups, raising their children together
without the daily presence of men. Conversely, during bust phases Helms contends that the men returned home and Miskitu families returned to patrilocal
residential patterns. Matrilocal residential practices, then, have played a central role in the Miskitu people's ability to adapt to market capitalism. (Helms
1970, 1971, 1976).

Miskitu men began leaving their communities to work on pirate and buc-caneer vessels in the latter half of the seventeenth century, and men's absences continued as the British militia took Miskitu men to fight against the Spanish to the west (Exquemelin 1981 [1685]:182). In the past two hundred years Miskitu men have continued to live away from their families for much of the year. Men have participated as migrant wage-laborers in various extractive industries, including mahogany, bananas, rubber, sarsaparilla, pine, turtles, and more recently spiny (rock) lobsters (C. Bell 1899; Conzemius 1932:147; Helms 1971:25; Nietschmann 1974, 1997; Newson 1986:283). Miskitu families adapted to these economies by living in matrilocal groups, a residential group composed of mothers, daughters, and sisters. Helms (1971: 23–28) argues that matilocality aided in the preservation of cultural practices: as the men became acculturated to outside economies and cultures, women remained society's "conservative cultural core." Charles Napier Bell describes a Miskitu village in the mid-1800s composed of women and children during the boom phase of the mahogany industry (C. Bell 1899:85–86). Matrilocality additionally pro-vided a way for Miskitu women to pass down language and culture to the children when the husband-fathers were of different ethnicities. In the early twentieth century Conzemius (1932:13) remarked that mixed-Miskitu chil-dren "always speak the language of the mother and grow up as Miskitu." This ethnohistoric data, along with my newer research, supports the notion that matrilocality has been an important factor in the Miskitu people's survival and ongoing proliferation.

In Helms's seminal work, she also characterized Miskitu society as a "pur-chase" society, in which foreign goods had become cultural necessities. She explains:

> The term purchase society is suggested because it emphasizes both the economic referent in general, and the specific aspect of that refer-ent which appears most important from the point of view of the local society, and towards which local adaptions will be directed, i.e., the need to obtain, to "purchase," through one means or another, foreign manufactured goods, which have acquired the status of cultural neces-sities. To be sure, something must be exchanged or sold in order to acquire these goods, but to the local population, that which is sold is merely a means to the all important end of purchasing. (Helms 1971:7)

More recent research by Baron Pineda provides a theory as to how the Miskitu people developed their emotional dependence on foreign goods. Pineda (2006:120–21) describes Puerto Cabezas, Nicaragua, during the banana industry boom. He reports that Standard Fruit Company paid their Miskitu and Creole employees in company scrip, which was used to purchase goods in company stores. During "company time," the stores imported necessities and luxury goods for the company managers and administrators and their U.S. families (mainly from New Orleans) living in Puerto Cabezas. Paying company scrip to Miskitu male laborers created a market for company goods and encouraged the men to spend all of their pay at company stores. Pineda (2006:21) states that payment in company scrip internalized a "consumer culture" for Miskitu workers in Puerto Cabezas.

Helms (1971) also contends that the boom and bust economy effected the emotional state of the Miskitu people. She reports that Asang residents had become both physically and emotionally dependent on store-bought goods when cash was plentiful, so after the bust they experienced feelings of helplessness because they could not access the cash and store-bought items that they so desired. Helms (1971:224–25) explains, "this feeling is not only expressed in their formal prayers, but also is often heard in their daily conversation: '*Dia daukaia; ilp apu; pruaia baman*' ('what's to be done; there is no help; we can only die')." The title of Bernard Nietschmann's article "When the Turtle Collapses, the World Ends" (1974) similarly conveys the fearful attitude men and women in Tasbapauni, Nicaragua, had regarding the potential bust in the green-sea-turtle industry. Similar to the lobster-diving occupation in Kuri, the turtle industry supported nearly all the families in Tasbapauni.

My research offers a study of social organization during a new and different boom economy. My work in Kuri presents new research from the Honduran Miskito Coast that highlights Miskitu society during the peak of the binational (Honduras-United States) lobster economy. Similar to Helms's predictions, men lived away from their homes on lobster boats while women bonded together to raise the children and share resources. Coastal residents seemed to be most happy when in the act of purchasing goods. Helms would attribute the differing postmarital residential patterns and distinct emotional states of individuals in Asang in the late 1960s and Kuri in the late 1990s to their being in different stages of the boom and bust economic model. This study supports Helms's boom and bust model, positing more continuity than disjuncture in Miskitu practices through time. However, my research in coastal Honduras reveals some new adaptations to the expanding market economy. Most significantly, female-centered domestic organization and commodified gender identities intensified during the long boom in the lobster economy. Kuri residents developed such a profound physical and emotional desire for cash that market-based capitalism now regulates behaviors and relationships between women and men. This contributes to understanding the interlinkages between global economic forces and indigenous kinship and gender identities.

My research also reveals more specifics about boom and bust economics along the north coast of the Río Plátano Biosphere Reserve. Oral histories and interviews with local elders prove that no true economic bust has occurred on the reserve's north coast, at least not since the north coast villages were settled one hundred years ago. When one industry collapsed, another seemed to replace it. From 1900 to the 1920s Honduran Miskitu men worked for foreign banana companies on the Río Plátano. From the 1920s to the 1960s men worked for various industries extracting rubber, animal hides, and sarsaparilla. Many men also worked in Belize in the 1920s and in Nicaragua in the 1950s and 1960s, cutting mahogany trees for North American companies. Deepwater lobster diving began in the early 1970s and continues today, along with an increase in shrimp and conch extraction. Ecotourism and drug trafficking have also begun on a minor scale in recent years.

During interviews with elders regarding village histories, I found that female-centered social organization and male absenteeism have existed in Kuri since the village was founded. David Dodds (1998:8–11) believes the boom and bust economy was less relevant on the north coast because of its role as a regional market center. This may be true, as Miskitu families originally left their upriver villages and moved to the coast at the beginning of the twentieth-century. Elders maintained that families moved to the coast because the women wanted to live closer to the stores that sold goods. Therefore, I contend that a more or less continuous consumer culture and boom phase of the economy has characterized coastal Miskitu villages since they were settled.

While evidence suggests that no major economic busts have occurred on the north coast of the Plátano biosphere, seasonal unemployment does create a yearly mini-cycle of boom and bust behaviors. The lobster industry provides steady work to the male divers only from August through March. The eight-month diving season is followed by a veda, or four-month moratorium on lobster diving. During the veda, little cash is present and no merchandise boats bring goods to the north coast. Many women fall into a dreary emotional state and have withdrawal symptoms because of their inability to purchase familiar goods. With no money available, many women accustomed to buying food from stores daily feel helpless trying to feed their children. They subsist on the few agricultural items that their husbands and other relatives provide from upriver, yet little dietary diversity exists during the veda. Some women opt to join their husbands and family in agricultural camps upriver, living off of the land and counting the weeks until the diving season begins again. These manifestations of a boom and bust mentality reaffirm Helms's (1969, 1971) characterization of Miskitu society as a "purchase" society.

Fieldwork and Methods

Following in the tradition of extensive, long-term ethnographic fieldwork in cultural anthropology, this study results from field research that took place in the Río Plátano Biosphere Reserve in 1991 (six months), 1995 (six weeks), 1997–1998 (18 months), and 2001 (six weeks). I mainly lived in the coastal village of Kuri and traveled from there to other villages in the Plátano biosphere. Field research combines participant observation with household interviews and the collection of linguistic data.[1] I used my linguistic abilities in English, Spanish, and Miskitu—I had a base knowledge of Miskitu when I arrived for my dissertation research in 1997–1998, and I continued to study and practice speaking the Miskitu language in Kuri. Learning Miskitu benefited this fieldwork because many women, especially the older ones, spoke only basic Spanish.

My main hypothesis is that during the long boom in the lobster economy matrifocality and commodified gender identities developed in coastal villages like Kuri. The research methods for this book have two components, focusing on (1) domestic organization and (2) gender and sexuality. To study domestic organization, my field research combines participant observation with household interviews. I became close friends with members of Kuka Denecela's matrilocal group and was considered family (*tasbaya taihka*) as I detailed their everyday life through my interactions with them. I first completed a census of the village, and then I went on to conduct interviews with Kuka Denecela's matrigroup. From there, I continued carrying out interviews throughout the community. In total, I completed two interviews with every woman of childbearing age in each Kuri household.

To study gender identities in Kuri, I combined participant observation with the collection of sociolinguistic data, especially songs and incantations.

Ultimately, I aim to show that gender and sexual identities have become commodified in coastal villages like Kuri. Kevin Yelvington (1995, 2006) recognizes how gender, race, and class identities historically were commodified in Caribbean society. This commodification of bodies developed with chattel slavery in the early colonial era and continues today, as young women work in factories and are valued for their nimble fingers, subservience, and ability to work long hours. On the Miskito Coast, Miskitu men are considered a cheap labor force, valued for their diving skills along with their ability to withstand life-threatening working conditions. My research demonstrates that when a diver is killed at sea, his family is paid a sum of money based on the diver's market value. In his critique of political economic theory, Karl Marx states that commodification occurs when something not previously considered in economic terms, such as gender identity, is assigned a market value (K. Marx 1997). My analysis points to a similar commodification of men's gender identities.

Marx's idea of commodity fetishism also seems relevant to the north coast of the Plátano biosphere. For Marx, commodity fetishism has to do with relationships between people in capitalist societies, where commodity production runs rampant—social relationships become transformed into relationships between people and commodities or people and money. I argue that a kind of commodity fetishism has taken place on the north coast of the Plátano biosphere. No commodities are produced locally for market, but goods shipped in from larger cities have altered, mystified, and commercialized relationships between Miskitu women and men. This book will illustrate that women's desire for cash and cash-based commodities regulates their behaviors toward men.

To further explore the development of monetized relationships between women and men in Kuri, I collected sociolinguistic and ethnographic data concerning lobster-diver songs, sexual magic, the water spirit, and transactional sexual relations. Buzo lawana (lobster-diver songs) serve as a window through which to view the men's identities—the song texts show that men are considered economic resources, or "money trees" (lalah dusa), by the women. The women's use of praidi saihka (sexual magic) illustrates that women chant incantations to increase their chance of garnering the men's wages. The liwa mairin, or Mermaid, a water spirit, is believed to seduce men with her lobster resources and then take their lives in exchange. Data about mairin mana describe the way women trade money for sexual relations with the divers. Central to my argument is that many Afro-Caribbean identities and social practices have taken hold in Miskitu society during the long boom in the lobster economy.

The sociolinguistic data were collected through tape recording, transcription, and translation. The song and incantation texts also contribute directly to the study of verbal art in the indigenous Americas (Sammons and Sherzer 2000; see also Minks 2008). Buzo songs, as locals refer to them, are both older and newer songs that men sing about their lives. As a genre of music, the songs are part of a broader category of Miskitu music called, *tasbaya lawanka* (earthly or profane songs), which locals distinguish from *dawan lawanka* (church or sacred songs). Today's quintessential buzo songs commonly lament the physical and emotional hardships that lobster divers endure—many divers are injured, paralyzed, or killed while deepwater diving; their lives are also sad because they live on boats, away from home and loved ones. The saddest songs, perhaps, are those that refer to the way women use and abuse men for their money.

Almost all lobster-diver songs presented in this book were recorded at my house in Kuri. Wilintin Suárez and Eusebio Guevara, two of the best musicians and singers in the region, sang and played guitars while my small but efficient Sony recorder–cassette player taped them. The musicians were not sure about many of the song titles and also improvised with lyrics of old standards. I came to realize that they rarely performed a song the same way twice. Wilintin and Eusebio, who both lived in Kuri, had time to dedicate to the recording sessions. Both men had been injured while diving the previous lobster season and more than welcomed the money that I offered them.

When the out-of-work divers occasionally wanted to drink beer and had no money to buy their own, they would approach my house with a false timidity. Wilintin, the one I knew the best, would ask with a wink and a nod, "Laura, do you want to record lobster-diver songs tonight?" I gladly would give them 200 lempiras (about U.S. $14) to buy beer, locally made rum, and usually a guitar string or two. Two or three of their friends joined in as backup singers, played percussion with a metal pot lid and spoon, and helped change batteries and cassettes. The recording sessions usually turned into late-night parties at my house, and neighbors who had overheard the mayhem the night before would come over early the next morning to listen to the tape.

I also paid Wilintin and Eusebio 300 lempiras (U.S. $22) apiece after the tape was finished. It was important to the divers that I made and gave each of them multiple copies of each of the cassettes we recorded. With no radio stations in this part of Honduras that played Miskitu music, the tapes became hot commodities, and bootlegs (copies of copies) soon appeared. Years later, in

2004, I was taken aback when I heard tracks that had been recorded at my house in 1997–1998 being played on Radio Miskut in Puerto Cabezas, Nicaragua. In 2001 I visited the coast and collected songs from another Miskitu musician and diver, Silin Tailor. By the time I returned to the coast in 2010, Honduran Miskitu professional singers Romel Cruz and Larry Morales had made CDs of their music, which I bought in the market in the nearest city, La Ceiba. Many of the songs on the CDs also recount the life of lobster divers.

Praidi saihka (literally, Friday's medicine), is a subcategory of earthly medicine (*tasbaya saihka*) that deals specifically with plant- and animal-based cures.[2] Praidi saihka manipulates the emotions and actions of others and is one of the most guarded realms of Miskitu cultural practice. The incantations used to render praidi saihka potions into supernatural remedies are part of a highly stylized genre of spoken Miskitu that differs from everyday speech. Instead of speaking with an interlocutor, women engage a supernatural other, similar to reciting a prayer. Women speak in a rhythmic, low-pitched voice, often semi-chanting. When they are home alone, women may put a sheet or towel over their head to ensure complete privacy during their prayer time, just in case passers-by or children spy through the walls or floorboards.

Locals vehemently deny using these potions for three reasons. First, the fear of "black magic" runs high in Kuri. A person who discovers someone is making a potion will become fearful that he or she will be the victim of this potion and may retaliate with a poison in return, starting a cycle of revenge murders. Second, Kuri residents who self-identify as Christians deny using magic potions, as the Moravian, Catholic, and Pentecostal Churches teach their congregations that potions are sacrilegious and sinful. Finally, elders contend that if someone discovers you using a potion on them, the potion is rendered ineffective. Additionally, the more educated Miskitu may claim not to believe in these "folk" practices. For all of these reasons, Kuri residents do not talk openly about sexual magic—the discourse is shrouded in secrecy.

During fieldwork, whenever I tried to broach the subject of praidi saihka with Kuka Denecela and her daughters they put me off. Discussing these matters, they believed, was dangerous and irresponsible. I remember trying to joke with Kuka Denecela's grandchildren, telling them that Kuka was going to teach me praidi saihka. Kuka came out from behind the house and pinned me against the wall, her thick hands around my neck. She glared down at me, asking, "Did I hear you mention praidi saihka again?," giving me a chance to lie. From under her grip I mouthed, "No, Kuka." She released me and muttered, "I didn't think so." Not wanting to complicate my relationships with the women in Kuka Denecela's matrigroup, I worked with Kuka Meri, a grandmother from another village, to gather information on the subject of praidi saihka. Doña Meri, a respected elder from New Jerusalem (just west of Kuri), frequently collaborated with MOPAWI (the local development organization), providing traditional knowledge regarding plant cures, songs, and dances. Kuka Meri taught me the names of the praidi saihka potions, the situations in which to use them, and their recipes and incantations. I was then able to weave my understanding into conversations with the women of Kuka Denecela's matrigroup and of greater Kuri. No one wanted the responsibility of teaching me about praidi saihka; once I knew about it, however, the local women (especially the younger ones) talked openly about how these potions affected their daily lives. I found that the more that I progressed in learning the Miskitu language, the more these realms of Miskitu cultural practice opened to me.

FEMINIST ETHNOGRAPHY

My study views Miskitu women as primary actors in their society. This contrasts with most of the published social science literature, which focuses on Miskitu political and military leaders, a theme that accentuates masculine Miskitu actors within the context of the nation-state. Yet, in what way does my research qualify as feminist ethnography? By Bruce Knauft's (1996:222) definition, feminist ethnography (1) gives voice to marginalized women, (2) examines female contestations of the male patriarchy, (3) uses an experimental writing style, and (4) provides a transformative personal experience for the researcher. First, my research recovers women's voices in a marginalized place—a small community in coastal Honduras. Women's voices bring to light the more feminine and multi-vocalic aspects of Miskitu identity.

Second, this research examines female contestations of patriarchal structures in coastal Miskitu society. Research demonstrates that Miskitu women utilize strategies like mairin mana and sexual magic to contest the male-dominated lobster economy. This analysis asks whether Miskitu women's strategies are viable forms of resistance to patriarchal economic structures in Miskitu society, where only men have access to wages through the lobster industry. While overstating the trivial as a form of resistance is problematic in anthropology today (M. Brown 1996; Goldstein 2003), viewing mairin mana and sexual magic within this paradigm should not be ignored just because it may be overused. Rather, the concept of resistance appears to offer a rich and useful way to understand Miskitu women's voices (see chapter 6).

Third, this ethnography at times employs an experimental writing style, presenting several short stories or narratives as well as song and incantation texts. The stories from my field journals are meant to bring the Miskitu people and my research to life (Richardson 1990). Some stories were written during my original travels to the region in 1991, when I first arrived in Kuri with my geographer husband Peter Herlihy. At that time I had finished my MA in anthropology at Louisiana State University and was scouting sites for future doctoral research. Other stories were written when I returned for an extended winter break in 1995, during my dissertation fieldwork in 1997–1998, and during a return visit in the summer of 2001. The stories contextualize my life as an ethnographer in the village and serve as confessionals that disclose the way I lived with Kuka Denecela's matrigroup over a ten-year period.

Feminist ethnographers today revalue travel accounts written by early anthropologists' wives who accompanied their husbands to the field. They identify the writing style as a uniquely feminine way of writing—the woman writer is often part of the story, she uses reflexivity, and she may blend fact and fiction (Behar and Gordon 1995).[3] Kamala Visweswaran (1997) maintains that feminist ethnography has evolved since the days of travel journals because today's feminist ethnographers produce narratives about the fieldworker's activities and involvement with the research question at hand. My stories are intended to deal directly with gender and power relations, highlighting female-centered domestic organization and monetized gender identities. Because I am a woman, while I was in a society with strict gendered divisions of labor I was privy to the personal stories of the women in a way that I was not with the men. Especially because I was married and my husband was gone most of the time, my life had many parallels with the Miskitu women's. They usually talked openly with me about their husbands and even began teaching me their secret ways of controlling the men and their money.

GIRLS' NIGHT OUT IN MOSKITIA

I returned alone to Kuri for six weeks in November–December 1995, taking an extended winter break from my doctoral program in Lawrence, Kansas. Being there alone for a relatively short time, I decided to live in Delfina's house. During these weeks I bonded with the other "men-less" Miskitu women in the village, who jokingly called themselves piarkas *(widows). Most of their husbands and boy-friends were working offshore on lobster boats. We even had what I called "girls' night out" to Two Man Disco, a recently opened hot spot in Utla Almuk. The disco was a raised, one-room wooden structure with a generator-powered strobe light system, refrigerator-freezer, and jam box.*

Most of the women who participated in the girls' nights out were forbidden to go by their husbands. One dark and moonless night I had a short conversation with Ilabia's husband, Mindel, a lobster diver who had just returned to shore.

Mindel, whom was normally shy if not a bit despondent, asked me point blank, "Did you go to Two Man Disco, sister-in-law [lamlat]?"

"Yes, brother-in-law [maisaia]," I returned.

"Who did you go with?" he continued. Out of nowhere, I felt a sudden throng of a wrist in my back. Ilabia, running to join our conversation, had poked me, a signal not to say her name.

"I went with Delfina to sell rum to the divers," I lied. Women of the same matrigroup, I had learned, were expected to lie for each other, especially to their husbands, who may beat their wives for talking, drinking, and dancing with other men.

Other women also began to include me in their marital deceptions. One sister in the matrigroup took advantage of my presence and used me for a series of coverups from her husband. Whenever she wanted to meet her boyfriend, she told her husband that I had asked her to accompany me to another village to record tambako songs (performed only at Christmas time) for my research. My allegiance to this woman at times grew thin, especially since Peter and I were friends with her husband. And we much preferred the husband to the boyfriend. A low point came when I was forced to stay the night with her in the neighboring town of New Jerusalem, just west of Kuri. I had no choice but to sleep in a stranger's house and share a bed with three children (only two were potty trained) while this woman slept with her boyfriend on a mattress in the adjoining cookhouse. As the soft rays of daybreak rolled across the sea we walked home together along the beach, away from the village path where the eyes of speculation would be upon us.

RETURN OF THE LOBSTER DIVER

When a diver returned from sea, women in the village rushed to the diver's house and warned his wife by knocking on the side wall. In a hushed voice they would say, "Maiam balan" (Your husband's back). My husband, Peter, passed through the village to visit me about every two weeks toward the end of my 1997–1998 fieldwork season. Because my situation was similar to their own, women in Kuri began warning me when Peter had arrived, as if he were a returning buzo.

One Sunday night at Tomasa's bodega, I was drinking a beer with Alan (Peter's former guide). Ilabia ran up the steps. She looked terrified and tried to talk in a low voice, "Sister Laura, your husband just walked into Kuri and he's looking for you. I told him you were at church."

Tomasa, visibly scared for me, said, "Go quickly! Run!"

There was no way to explain to the sisters that Peter would not be mad at me for being out of the house or for drinking a beer with a man—it was only our guide, Alan. For them, a Miskitu husband's scolding or beating would be expected. They assumed Peter would do the same to me. The next day the sisters perused my body parts for bruises, stupefied by the lack of evidence regarding my punishment.

A week later Peter and his team of consultants and indigenous personnel arrived unexpectedly. When their boat docked in Tampa Tingni lagoon (bordering Kuri) in the middle of the afternoon, I was inside Kuka's house, participating in a private healing party with music, beer, and dancing. The healing party revolved around a new age suhkia (shaman) who claimed to have astrological prowess. Her name, Planeta, reflected her dubious reputation as a charlatan and swindler. Many husbands would be infuriated by their wife partaking in such wanton, hedonistic behavior, especially in the middle of the day. To make matters worse, Kuka's house was located next to the Moravian church, where the pastor could potentially see or hear us.

Once the news hit Kuka's house that Peter had arrived, Tomasa's hand pulled me out to the veranda. Even for the always alegre or lilia Tomasa, this was no laughing matter. She poured a complete tub of water over my head and instructed me, "Tell him you were bathing." Kuka, evidently in cahoots with Tomasa, joined us and wrapped me in a towel. As I climbed down the stairs, Kuka doused me from behind with some of her cologne, a last-minute attempt to hide the stench of debauchery.

From that day on, I was never caught off-guard again by my husband's arrival. As I forged alliances along the coast, I began to receive messages from friends telling me where Peter was along the trail or waterways to Kuri. Women sent their children to keep me updated on his latest whereabouts. And then the moment would come when I would hear open-hand thumps on the split-wood walls, accompanied by the final words of warning from one of my muihki (sisters): "Maiam balan" (Your husband's back).

The fourth feature of feminist ethnography, following Knauft (1996:222), is that it should provide the researcher with a transformative personal experience. In my case, this also held true. The relationships that I formed in the field with Kuka Denecela and her daughters propelled me toward becoming a mother. Over the seven-year period (1991–1998) of my presence and fieldwork in Kuri, most of the women I interacted with were mothers. I watched these women daily in their child-rearing activities and learned what motherhood meant to them. While I could not directly understand motherhood when I did my field-work and data collection, I got pregnant two months after returning from my dissertation fieldwork and wrote my dissertation while I was pregnant and as a new mom. On a return trip to Kuri in 2001, I brought my then-two-year-old daughter Simone to Kuri. My collection of field data concerning mother-daughter relations was more in the abstract, but the analysis of the data was done in the throes of new motherhood and seemed to blend with real life.

Head of Household

Entering the village in March 1997 felt like returning home; as I reacquainted myself with the children, it struck me that I had watched them grow up, having held them as infants in 1991, played with them on the beach in 1995, and now was seeing them as schoolchildren. Over the course of my stay Peter and I paid to build a fairly large house by local standards. Built on posts with a rough hardwood floor, split-palm walls, and a roof of tin, the house had a balcony in the front and, on the side, a bathhouse and a small porch with a staircase. Because it was raised up high like a birdhouse, I could pick mangoes off the tree from my back window.

The house stood on Delfina's beachfront property and tied into the patio for her own burgeoning matrigroup. Peter and I would own the house but not the land or the remains of a dooryard orchard of coconut, cashew, berry, mango, and other fruit trees that surrounded it. Delfina made me responsible for protecting her fruit trees, and I often had to yell at passers-by from my balcony, "Leave my cashews alone," especially to the children who snatched what they could while walking along the east-west trail that passes through the dooryard gardens of the community.

After moving into the new house, I acquired a new, heightened status as a female head of household. In many ways I identified with what it meant to be a buzo wife. By this time my grant had ended and I relied on my husband's sal-ary. Peter was away, working as a consultant for the German firm Gesellschaft fur Agrarprojekte (GFA) to design a conservation project for the Río Plátano

Figure 46. Laura's House, Kuri,
by M. Kendrid, age ten

Biosphere Reserve. Similar to a buzo, Peter passed through the village about every two weeks, usually bringing me money (lempiras and U.S. dollars). Even though I had a lifestyle similar to a buzo maia's (a lobster-diver's wife), I had still not achieved full adult female status in the eyes of the Kuri women—I was not yet a mother. They thought it strange for a woman of my age (then thirty-five) with no medical problems to not have children. They often asked me in bewilderment, "Who hauls your water? Who sweeps your floors? Who do you send to the store?"

Delfina solved this problem by lending me three boys from her compound to live with me—Marcos and Bujeron (both twelve years old) and Ovni (Bujeron's four-year-old brother). The boys kept me company, protected me, and worked for me—hauling water, sweeping floors, and running errands to the store. At night they would spread their sheets and sleep on the wood floor. Marcos was an orphan and Bujeron and Ovni were the children of Ilabia and Mindel (introduced in a previous story), who had recently divorced and left Kuri. The parents, after later divorcing, had deserted their four children knowing that Delfina and her husband, Siksto, would support them and make sure they finished elementary school.

Marcos, Bujeron, and all of the children of the matrigroup called me Anti, but Ovni (pronounced Opni), the youngest boy who lived with me, called me Mama or Yapti. I was especially nurturing to this extremely small four-year-old. Ovni and I became a special unit—he accompanied me almost everywhere on my hip. The locals yelled out to me, "Put him down, he's too old," as other children his age were expected to do chores such as carrying laundry and water to and from the well. They explained to me that Ovni appeared younger than his years due to the fact that he was an orphan, a belief that extended to all abandoned children. Kuri locals thought of Ovni as an especially pitiable orphan; they pointed out to me, while laughing, that even his name begged ridicule—Ovni was the acronym in Spanish for UFO (objectos volantes no identificados)—because he usually orbited around the village with no supervision.[4]

With three children, a house, and a husband supporting me from afar, my status as a mother and female head of household emerged. My metamorphosis into someone with gravitas added to my friendships with the sisters and other local women and to my understanding as an anthropologist. By the end of my stay my days were filled with caring for children, socializing with an expanding group of sisters, and trying to fit in time to do interviews.

The Feminist Ethnographic Dilemma

Nancy Scheper-Hughes (1992) defines feminist ethnography as ethnography that is both socially engaged and ethically based. Socially engaged feminist ethnography focuses on applied topics that actually help women improve their lives. Ethically based feminist research methods are designed to minimize the power difference between the researcher and the researched. My research does not measure up to Scheper-Hughes's criteria for feminist ethnography—it is not politically activistic, nor do I use collaborative or participatory research methods to empower local female researchers. Still, development organizations could employ my data to make better-informed decisions about projects for Plátano biosphere women; and I do consider more-traditional research methods (participant observation, interviews, and the collection of oral texts) to be ethical, while recognizing that these methods do not readily train Miskitu women in data collection and analysis. Two notable feminist anthropologists have called into question whether doing feminist ethnography is even possible. Judith Stacey (1988:6) doubts it can be. She defines feminist ethnography as work that is sensitive to power differences and hierarchal relations in the field. She believes that the relationship between two women in the field, a (white) researcher-subject and a (brown) researched-object, reproduces the same hierarchal relations that feminists object to in postcolonial societies around the world.

HOLY WEEK IN LIWA RAYA

Kuka Denecela's entire matrilocal compound retreated upriver to Liwa Raya during Holy Week. Delfina alone stayed in Kuri to who watched over her "businesses" and the family's houses. When we arrived in Liwa Raya, Kuka Denecela's other daughters, Ilabia, Enemecia, and Tomasa, were fishing in a cutoff oxbow lake across the river, catching dinner for the barbecue and fish fry planned for that night.

An hour passed. The sisters ascended the bluff drenching wet, balancing buckets on their heads. They had waded and then swum across the river in their clothes. "Where are your fish, Laura?" Enemecia taunted me as she caught me looking up at what I hoped was our dinner. "Laura," she continued, "how are you going to feed Alan and Peter?"

"You have to learn how to cook or Peter's gonna leave you," Tomasa chimed in, walking two steps behind Enemecia.

Holding up the rear, Ilabia added, "The least you can do is help cook."

Once again, as would happen frequently over my stay, my gender role came into question. With nothing to look forward to but burning eyes and scorched fingers, I penetrated the hearth. Attempting to make the sisters laugh, I said, "Enemecia, you're just jealous because I have two men and you don't have any."

Enemecia squared off with me and looked infuriated. Alan was still a painful subject for her.

Alan stepped in, trying to diffuse the situation by making another joke, "Enemecia, a woman in the U.S. doesn't know how to work—she is an adornment in the house."

"Is that true, Laura?" Enemecia stared me down. Turning toward the fire, she muttered under her breath, "Give me a ticket then . . . I wanna go."

I felt a twinge down my spine. Here I was trying to bond with my "sistas," but what, after all, did Enemecia and I have in common?

When Enemecia said, "Give me a ticket, I wanna go," she implicitly expressed the feminist ethnographic dilemma—the unequal relationship between me, a wealthy *meriki mairin* (North American woman, or gringa) who was socially and economically entitled to be an interloper in her world, and her, a poor indigenous woman who may never leave Honduras.

Subject Positionality

Lila Abu-Lughod (1990), who disagrees with Stacey (1988), contends that feminist ethnography can indeed exist and flourish if researchers clarify their own subject positionality (see also Haraway 1988).[5] I will take a brief moment to sum up and clarify my own subject positionality in order to deconstruct a presumed objectivity and reveal the lenses through which I view and filter the Miskitu world: I am a married, white, female anthropologist, a *meriki mairin*; I lived in a village controlled by women and aim to show the central role that Miskitu women play in daily village life and in larger cultural processes. Some feminist ethnographers, such as Ruth Behar (1993), go to great lengths to describe who they are as people and how they relate to the female subjects in their research. Although not offering as much detail as Behar, I feel compelled to tell readers about two important moments in my life that help describe how I came to study on the Miskito Coast. One moment corresponds to when I discovered anthropology, and the other has to do with getting married. My smart but sarcastic girlfriends, who poke fun at my native Mississippi Delta culture's class and gender identities, sum up these major events in my life with two statements: "I didn't want to be a debutante, so I ran away to the rainforest to live with the Indians." And "I followed a boy."

Running Away to the Rain Forest

I grew up in a female-dominated family in New Orleans and attended an all-girls, private school in the Garden District. But truth be told, I grew up behind two brothers, was a tomboy, and always got along better with boys. Another anomaly from my social group was that I spent more time than my peers with the Other, which in New Orleans meant African Americans. I interacted with them daily, to my chagrin, as domestics and support staff—at home, at school, at restaurants, and at the country club.[6] I was commonly MIA from the big table, having entered and come to preferred backroom conversations. This was a purely social preference rather than any conscious political statement. Yet I was willingly bribed into making my debut in exchange for a trip to Spain. Thereafter I returned to the Crescent City to attend Tulane for my undergraduate degree (BA 1986) and live close to home. But as I followed through on my side of the debutante bargain, I realized that I could never live up to my socialite mother's expectations. During this angst-ridden moment in my life, I discovered anthropology at Tulane. The anthropology building, at that time on Audubon Street, was the only academic building on sorority and fraternity row, sitting next door to the Kappa Kappa Gamma house, where Ellie, my little sister, best friend, and rival, was an active member. I was not in a sorority, but I respected the Greeks commitment to planning, giving, and attending parties.

I was more drawn to the intriguing people coming out of the anthropology building, speaking in exotic languages and wearing colorful textiles. Convinced that the subject matter would be interesting, too, I enrolled in my first few classes and tried to fit in. My MO was to dress like a hippie-artist type and pretend that it was not me in the white dresses appearing almost weekly in the Vivant section of the Times-Picayune. *The secretaries in the department, though, found me out during Carnival season.[7] The secretaries pinned newspaper clippings of me as Queen of Athenians (my daddy was Captain of the Krewe) on the bulletin board. Anthropology student by day, debutante by night, I was mostly accepted by the Tulane anthropologists although not taken very seriously, especially since I was gregarious (i.e., did not act like an introverted academic) and had what they considered to be a southern accent. I soon realized that I was filling the role of native informant for the department, as almost all of the graduate students and teachers were Yankees (or what the local minority population at Tulane refer to as intellectual carpet-baggers). But I did not mind playing the role of native informant.*

I sat by Professor Munro Edmonson's side during his classes, laughing at his jokes, lighting his cigarettes, and sometimes taking notes. Professor Judith Maxwell, who commonly spoke K'achik'el around the department and dressed in Maya drag, became my personal favorite and still to this day is my hero; I took six of her classes, practically stalking her on campus (thank you, Judy, for never calling the campus police). And I still remember the day I walked shoulder to shoulder through the Tulane quadrangle with the renowned Mayanist ethnoarchaeologist Victoria Bricker. Dr. Bricker, with her white cat-eye glasses and hair in a tight bun, sized me up immediately. Cutting straight to the bone, she said, "You know, Laura, there's more to anthropology than getting along with the natives."

Hmmm. This gave me pause.

Even a decade later, during my fieldwork on the Miskito Coast, Dr. Bricker's words continued to haunt me. As days, weeks, and months flew by, I felt like I had not collected any data or made much progress on my research project. Yet I did get along well with the "natives." In fact, I was having the time of my life on the Miskito Coast. Although it drove my husband bonkers, I reveled in having so many visitors in my house on a daily basis. Also, as a young woman newly married to a slightly older, rather macho guy, I was having trouble adjusting to my sudden change in identity and status. The Miskitu women in Kuri unwittingly helped me through this. Infectiously strong, their primary identities seemed derived not from their status as wives or girlfriends but more from the roles they played as mothers, daughters, and sisters. I could definitely relate to these women; they were outgoing and irreverent, self-confident and assertive, talked slightly loud, and were inclined to have nightly parties in their homes. Just when I needed it most, I had finally found my sorority.

Following a Boy

Another major life-changing event for me was when I met my Yankee husband from upstate New York. We met on a Louisiana State University (LSU) field trip to Mexico. I was an LSU master's student in anthropology, on my way to complete a summer of field research in the Tepoztlán (Morelos, Mexico) marketplace. To save money, I joined a group of about twenty geographers (filling two large, white vans) en route to Querétero for the 1989 Conference of Latin American Geographers (CLAG). Peter was also on the field trip, having finished his PhD through LSU's geography department. He lived near Baton Rouge in Hammond and worked as an assistant professor at Southeastern Louisiana University (SLU). The group of mainly male geographers was quite entertaining, and I especially hit it off with one of them. With each new day, I would prolong my departure from the van, eventually deciding to attend the CLAG meeting with the group. Once the vans headed north for home, I finally got off in central Mexico to begin my research project. Peter, as the story goes, jumped ship somewhere close to the border and came back to look for me. He eventually found me in San Miguel de Allende. We went together to the Huichol region in the Sierra Madres of Jalisco, Durango, and Nayarit, just in time for their yearly peyote (Lophophora Williamsii) ceremony. The adventure gave us plenty of stories to tell at our wedding rehearsal dinner, about the Huichol cacique who wanted to arrest us, but the jail was full, and about how Peter had to negotiate with the cacique, offering him just one six-pack of beer to not make me his peyote festival wife.

Back in Louisiana Peter and I continued to "date"; mostly it was he who drove from Hammond to my apartment in Baton Rouge, usually with a gallon of White Russian daiquiris for me and my fellow graduate-school roommate. The courtship behavior that I describe regarding Peter following me (girls take note) did not endure. Soon after we were married, it became clear that it would be me who would follow him, especially as his career and paycheck from SLU and, later, the University of Kansas (KU) were what paid the bills. But for me, a striving ethnographer, there were many plusses to tagging along behind a field-oriented, Latin Americanist geographer. With no kids in tow as of yet, I accompanied him around Central America on almost every project he completed. And once he was hired in the geography department at KU in Lawrence, I was able to enter and eventually graduate (2002) from the KU PhD program in anthropology.

Being married to Peter, a cultural geographer who specializes in indigenous rainforest peoples, also has greatly influenced my field research. In fact, it was he who first took me to the Miskito Coast, as his girlfriend in 1990 to the Tawahka Sumu region along the middle Río Patuca and then as his new bride in 1991 to the Río Plátano Biosphere Reserve north coast, where I would begin this project. Ironically, I had followed a man to embark on my feminist ethnographic research project. Without him I probably would never have worked in such a remote region, and as a single woman I would have encountered many more difficulties doing research. Somehow directly related to all of this, I continue to find it difficult to incorporate Western feminism into my everyday life. Therefore, my study recognizes its own partial view of reality.

Donna Haraway (1988) and Sally Price (1993) warn female anthropologists who search for strong sisterhoods in foreign lands not to overstate their claims or project a "false harmony" on the societies they study.[8] Postmodernists (Clifford 1986:104; Marcus and Fischer 1986:58) similarly critique the feminist ethnographer's less than objective eye, claiming that their flawed ethnographies equate culture with women, the mirror image of earlier ethnographies written by men that ignored women (Visweswaran 1997). Keeping these admonitions in mind, I aim to focus on both men's and women's power and gendered identities in Kuri. When I first began research in Kuri, I emphasized what I then called the women's "female autonomy." My later research focused more on how men maintain their authority as society's main breadwinners and how women, in their everyday lives, use strategies to contest the male-dominant lobster economy. The truth of the matter is that when I lived in Kuri during my 1991 field season, I overestimated Miskitu women's power in society, but during later research (in 1997–1998) I fully realized the power that men maintain as the main breadwinners in north coast villages. Because I recognized the contradictory power relations in Kuri, I situate the study within the literature on matrifocality.

PART II

Social Economies
of Power

CHAPTER THREE

Village of Women

Mothers, Daughters, and Sisters

This chapter describes Miskitu social organization during the boom phase of the lobster economy. The first part describes matrilocal residential practices and matrifocal domestic organization in Kuri. The second section compares Helms's data from the late 1960s to my own data from the late 1990s to illustrate the loss of the patrilineal descent group (kiamp) in Kuri and the trend toward matriliny. Miskitu matrilocal residential patterns that co-occur with patrilineal descent have been documented previously in the published literature (Dennis 2004; García 1996a,b; Peter Espinoza 2006). My research in Kuri presents a case study of Miskitu village organization, documenting Miskitu matrilocality, matrifocality, and matriliny for the first time in the ethnographic literature. This may demonstrate a more Caribbean domestic organization among the Plátano Miskitu people.

Raymond T. Smith (1956) coined the term "matrifocal" to refer to black Caribbean families in British Guyana that live in consanguineal households and practice postmarital matrilocal residence, in which couples live near the wife's family after marriage. Gonzalez (1970:1–2), building on Smith, notes that in matrifocal Garífuna families members of a woman's household usually consist of unmarried daughters and their children and at times unmarried sons; she also noted that senior women typically head households and play the leading role psychologically (see also Mohammed 1986; P. Scott 1995; Tanner 1974). Matrilocal residential practices were present in Kuri, but household composition differed from Garífuna families as reported by Gonzalez. Miskitu daughters moved out of their mother's household and into their own after having children. The daughters' households, however, were linked together by a senior woman, a grandmother, or kuka, who functioned as the psychological head of the matrigroup.

In my discussion of matrifocality in Kuri I borrow from Evelyn Blackwood's (2005) article "Wedding Bell Blues: Marriage, Missing Men, and Matrifocal Follies." Blackwood reviews the many different features of matrifocality noted in the literature and divides them into two main categories: *mother-centered families* and *low male salience*.[1] Blackwood identifies low male salience as "the missing men," in which the husband-father plays a limited role in the family (see also Strathern 2005). She argues that male absenteeism should not be a feature that marks matrifocality. According to Blackwood it is wrong to view women's power in matrifocal societies being caused by or contingent upon men's absence (see also Sanday 2002).[2] Blackwood would have to agree, however, that male absenteeism occurs at an accelerated rate in coastal Miskitu society. During Blackwood's (2000) own field research in a Sumatran community, she found that about 30 percent of the men were gone; whereas in Kuri, 90 percent of men over the age of thirteen were away from the village on a daily basis. Given this, I examine the influence of male absenteeism on domestic organization and gendered power in Kuri. In table 3 I separate the matrifocal features that I found in Kuri into Blackwood's categories of mother-centered families and low male salience.

TABLE 3. Matrifocal features in Kuri

MOTHER-CENTERED FAMILIES

    Matrilocality

    Mothers as household decision makers

    Senior women as family leaders

    Inheritance through the female line

    Motherhood highly valued

    Women's important role in healing and ritual activity

    Emphasis on matrilineal relatives

    Male absenteeism

    Female-headed households

    Serial monogamy (conjugal bond weak)

    Illegitimacy (outside children)[a]

    Adopted kin on the mother's side

    Male emigration/exogamy

[a]Illegitimate children are called "half siblings" in my analysis of household composition.

My research also proposes that Miskitu women are the primary transmitters of traditional practices and identity to the children (L. Herlihy 2007:145–46). Kuri women typically married men from outside of the region and sometimes, from a different ethnic group. As such, the women knew more than most men about village histories, genealogies, and local kinship relations. Most significantly, the women's husbands typically did not know the proper kinship terms of reference or understand reciprocity obligations among their wife's family. The senior women, or kukas, in the matrigroup were the local experts and enforcers of correct kinship and broader social and economic behaviors, and descent was increasingly traced through the female line. My argument is that Miskitu women have assumed positions of power in a matrilocal, matrifocal, and increasingly matrilineal society.

Matrilocality

Postmarital residence in Kuri was decidedly matrilocal; couples resided near the wife's family after marriage. In 1997 the village of Kuri (pop. 175) was geographically divided into five matrilocal groups that accounted for 88 percent of the households (twenty-two of twenty-five houses) (L. Herlihy 2007:135). Below is a Miskitu song performed by Wilintin Tejeda and Eusebio Guevara, narrated from the perspective of a *wahma* (young man) who wants to marry a *tiara* (young woman). The song text illustrates postmarital matrilocal residential practices: "I will give her a little house close to your home." The wahma sings to his potential future in-laws using the terms of reference *taihka* (father's sister or father's brother's wife) and *tahti* (father's sister's husband or father's brother). An older song, it may imply a previous preference for cross- or parallel-cousin marriage in Miskitu society. The prospective son-in-law reassures the young woman's parents that he will be a good provider, build a house for his wife, and buy small animals for her. We will later see that earning and giving resources to a woman is a fundamental component of Miskitu manhood (see chapter 5).

Taihka, taihka, tahti, tahti	Auntie, Auntie, Uncle, Uncle
Taihka taihka taihka,	Auntie, Auntie, Auntie
tahti tahti tahti	Uncle, Uncle, Uncle
luhpiam mairin yangra aikma kaka	if you give me your daughter
kalilka yabamni	I will give her chickens
kwirkuka yabamni	I will give her pigs
watla luhpia yabamni	I will give her a little house
man wampla lamara	close to your home

Mothers, daughters, and sisters form the core of the matrigroup, living near each other throughout their lives, and share in the reproductive work of raising the children. In Miskitu kinship terminology, cousins, brothers, and sisters are all called by the same terms, "muihki" (same sex, same generation) and "lakra" (different sex, same generation). With cousins raised together like siblings, many females play the role of mother to a child, including grandmothers, aunts, older sisters, and female cousins.

The social and economic ties between women of the matrigroup create the most enduring and important ties in Miskitu society (see also García 1996a, 1996b; Helms 1970, 1971; Peter Espinoza 2006). Using the paths between households, related women visited each other daily, and individual households of the matrigroup functioned like rooms of one greater house, bound together by a well in the center. The well served as the central social station, where related women held court, gossiped, and joked while washing clothes, bathing, and hauling water. Each residential compound formed a separate neighborhood, or *barrio*, with its own name, usually separated by dooryard gardens. The strong sense of solidarity between members of the matrilocal group, then, expresses itself through the presence of natural and manmade boundaries.

Matrilineal Inheritance

Matrilocality provides for the right of every daughter to settle on her mother's land. The land given to a daughter typically surrounds the mother's house and patio area. Eventually a group of homes for the sisters and their families would

FIGURE 17. A boy roasting cashews, Kuri (PHOTO CREDIT: Laura Herlihy)

FIGURE 18. A girl with cashew fruit in hand, Kuri (PHOTO CREDIT: Laura Herlihy)

encircle the mother's patio. Sons also have land rights, but following the post-marital pattern of residence men usually move near the wife's family.[3] Newly married Miskitu couples may live in the wife's parents' house until the husband accumulates enough money and resources to build a small house. Yet marriages are not considered real until the man builds his wife a home. Village residents refer to the home as, for example, "Tomasa watla" (Tomasa's house), assuming it to be the property of the wife.

Besides the land for a home, Kuri women also inherited fruit trees from their mothers. Dooryard orchards included coconut, mango, plum, breadfruit, and cashew trees. Women demonstrated their ownership of these trees as they scolded children who knocked down fruits with sticks and tried to sneak away with a sweet snack. Even after families sold their land and moved to another part of the village, they retained ownership of their trees and their fruit. Owners of trees came back seasonally to reclaim their fruit no matter who currently owned the land. Villagers told me about trees, "If you planted it, it's yours." Coconut trees (*kuku dusas*) provided important year-round fruit for

Kuri women. The women used coconut meat, water, and milk in their cooking three times a day, in rice, soups, or broths. Mothers typically planted a coconut tree with the birth of each female daughter. By the time the girl had children herself, the tree should be bearing fruit steadily. Many mothers pointed out trees to me, indicating which daughter would inherit them in the future. No mothers ever indicated that a coconut tree was for a son. After all, it is assumed that a son will move to his future wife's home.

Outside and Adopted Kin

My research in Kuri demonstrates that households include outside children, adopted children of the wife's sisters, and various other temporary boarders. Almost 40 percent of Kuri households in 1998 had half siblings as members. These half siblings resulted from previous marriages of the mother. Some 36 percent of Kuri households included adopted children. The majority of

Figure 49.
A tiara with an iron, Kuri
(photo credit: Laura Herlihy)

the children were girls who were adopted by their mother's sister or mother's mother. Adoptions could be temporary or last a lifetime but usually were not sanctioned by an authority higher than the matrigroup. It mattered little in which household you were raised; all descendants of the kuka inherited land and shared in subsistence, game meat, and other resources.[4] Adopted children grow up using dual systems of kinship, calling two or more women Mama or Yapti and assuming the corresponding terminology for all others in the two households. Thus, a child may call many women Mama throughout his or her life (see also Stack 1974). Children in Kuri were often given to their grandmothers or aunts, who took over as primary caregiver. Teenage girls were especially in demand to cook, wash clothes, and help with childcare responsibilities.

MOTHERHOOD HIGHLY VALUED

Nancy Tanner (1974:131–32) similarly argues that in matrifocal societies what is most important is that motherhood and the mother-child dyad are culturally valued. In the following song text, "Mama, Mama" a professional Miskitu singer named Romel Cruz describes the bond that men feel with their mothers. He sings from a son's perspective, stating that many men in his life can act as fathers but only one woman can be his mother (see also Bakewell 2010). From a child's perspective, the mother alone remains present in the household over a lifetime.

Mama, Mama	Mother, Mother
Mama, Mama	Mother, Mother
aisika nani ailal sa	there are many fathers
mama lika kumi	but just one mother

Motherhood and having many children are highly valued in Miskitu society. Young girls are socialized to become mothers at an early age, usually around ten. At this time a girl is given almost full responsibility for taking care of a baby or toddler, who is referred to as their *luhpia*, or child. By the time a girl is thirteen, she has finished school and is working in her mother's kitchen, supervising younger siblings. A young woman begins having romantic relationships around the age of fifteen or sixteen. Within a few years she will give birth, passing through the most important rite of passage for women. Data reveal that all women in Kuri over the age of eighteen are mothers.

FIGURE 20. Two girls, Kuri
(PHOTO CREDIT: Laura Herlihy)

FIGURE 21. A young mother with her baby,
Kuri (PHOTO CREDIT: Laura Herlihy)

Soon after having a child, married mothers usually move into their own homes. This integrates young mothers into social and sharing networks with other women in the matrigroup (see also Helms 1971). Claudia García (1996b:14) claims that Miskitu women's high level of power results from the roles they play as mothers and creators of ties between domestic units. Women gain status and power with the birth of each new child. The following verse of the Miskitu song "Arelita mairin" (Arelita woman, or Lady Arelita) reveals that those with children are considered to be wealthy:

Arelita mairin
Waikna nani aisika ritz na
    waikna
mairin nani aisika rits na
    waikna
tuktan nani aisika rits
    na waikna

Arelita woman
The parents of the men are
    millionaires
the parents of the women are
    millionaires
the parents of the children are
    millionaires

SOCIAL ECONOMIES OF POWER

Children serve as an economic resource within the matrigroup—female children help with cooking and other domestic chores and male children work the fields and earn money in wage-labor economies. On average in Kuri I found that women over the age of twenty-five have six children. However, Dodds (2001:96) shows that among two hundred indigenous women in the Plátano biosphere the average number of children per woman was eight. Kuri is one of the poorer settlements along the coast, where lobster diving is the only occupation. Poor health conditions exist for both men and women, who live far from health clinics and hospitals. Indeed, Kuri women have high rates of infant mortality, with about one-third of children dying within the first year. Due to the broader culture of lobster diving, women have begun to use birth control. Nurses in the region increasingly provide birth control to young men and women, including condoms and birth-control pills. This has given more Kuri women the opportunity to wait until their early twenties to become mothers.

Senior Women

As a young woman's family grows, her own mother becomes known as a kuka and takes over the position of senior woman in the matrilocal residential group. Each of the five matrigroups in Kuri revolved around the central house and patio of a kuka, including Kuka Denecela, Kuka Lyvian, Kuka Berihilda, Kuka Gladys, and one deceased kuka. A kuka is a grandmother, respected elder, landowner, and family health-care provider. She is both respected and feared by her descendants. Kuka Denecela's nickname was *kuka militar* (military grandmother) because she continually scolded her young and grown descendants. Others called her "doña CES" (CES is the acronym for the police force that worked in the region).

In Kuri I found that kukas are dominant in the family and make all household economic and child-rearing decisions. The kuka also maintains control over her sons-in-law by requiring them to perform physical labor for her, such as building her house or cleaning her well. Kuka Denecela once referred jokingly to her son-in-law as *albahuina* (literally, slave meat). The senior women exert power over their daughters' suitors, as Mark Jamieson (2000) notes, by teasing the young men (wahma) in public about their sexual prowess. Dennis (2004:92) points out that the Miskitu song "Sirpiki mairin" (My little woman) mentions that a mother, not a father, is the parent who chooses the daughter's suitor. Lyrics that I collected for a slightly different version of the song are below:

Sirpi luhpi mairin	**My little woman**
Sirpi luhpi mairin	My little woman
man kumi dukiamra	it's only for you
nara ba balri	that I came here
mamikam bui swiri ba daukan	your mother shamed me
tawi kli wari	so I went back again

FIGURE 22. Men cleaning a well, Kuri (PHOTO CREDIT: Laura Herlihy)

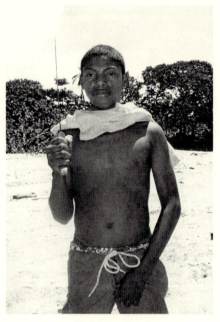

FIGURE 23. A wahma on the beach, Kuri (PHOTO CREDIT: Laura Herlihy)

WOMEN AS HEALERS

A Miskitu mother's main responsibility is keeping her children healthy. Women of the matrigroup share information in their role as caregivers. Together, they diagnose and treat their children's everyday illnesses and those caused by supernatural forces. Grandmothers possess valuable pharmaceutical knowledge and serve as the primary health-care providers in the matrigroup. The kuka is responsible for keeping her descendants emotionally, spiritually, and physically healthy. The kuka teaches her daughters plant-based remedies and prayers when one of their children falls ill. These remedies vary among families, and

SOCIAL ECONOMIES OF POWER

each matrigroup has its own specialized plant-based knowledge. Some women known for having exceptional healing skills are called suhkias (shamans), specialists who lived between the natural and supernatural worlds. Indeed, five out of seven suhkias were women along the Plátano biosphere's north coast. Parry Scott (1995:287) underscores that women's heightened role in "cultural and religious manifestations" is an important feature of matrifocality.

THE MISSING MEN

The tables below illustrate those who claim permanent residency in Kuri. Tables 4 and 5 omit one major group of villagers—the men are missing. Viewing the entire population by age (table 6) reveals that Kuri is mainly composed of women and children under twelve years of age. The Miskitu women in Kuri had their own expression for the phenomenon of the missing men: waikna apu, (without men). The expression has two meanings. When used in speech as a social category, "waikna apu" can mean either "single woman" or "married woman with no man present." Thus Kuri women differentiate little between a single woman and a married woman whose husband is working away from home. My broader interpretation of "female-headed household" below reflects local linguistic categories.

TABLE 4. Claimed population by sex, 1998

TOTAL POPULATION	175
Male	79
Female	96

Source: L. Herlihy 2007:138

TABLE 5. Claimed population by age and sex, 1998

AGE	SEX		TOTAL
	MALE	FEMALE	
5 and under	20	29	49
6–12	24	18	42
13–15	17	26	43
26–39	8	12	20
40–55	7	7	14
56–	3	4	7
Total	175		

Source: L. Herlihy 2007:138

TABLE 6. Actual population older than thirteen, by age and sex, 1998

AGE	SEX		TOTAL
	MALE	FEMALE	
13–25	0	26	26
26–29	0	12	12
40–55	3	7	10
56–	1	4	5
Total	53		

Source: L. Herlihy 2007:138

FEMALE-HEADED HOUSEHOLDS

Table 7 reveals that, in 1998, 40 percent of Kuri households (ten of twenty-five) had no man residing permanently in the husband-father role and another 44 percent (eleven of twenty-five) claimed as permanent members men who lived away from their home most of the year. Combining the two types of households reveals that more than 80 percent of households in Kuri (twenty-one of twenty-five) were headed by a woman. Helen Safa (2005:315) argues that female-headed households are "a statistical indicator of the degree of matrifocality in society."

TABLE 7. Household composition

	1991	1998
Total households	22	25
Female head (waikna apu)	19	21
Husband away working	11	11
Single mother	8	10

Source: L. Herlihy 2007:138

The Centro de Estudios e Información de la Mujer Mulitétnica (CEIMM 2008:4) reports that 20 percent of Miskitu households in Nicaragua's North Atlantic Autonomous Region are female headed. Kuri's higher percentage can be attributed to the lobster economy and to the fact that no other occupations are available for men. During the 1997–1998 lobster-diving season, thirty-one of thirty-five men in Kuri were employed as canoemen (*cayuqueros*) or divers. The divers usually took two, twelve-day trips to sea every month, and in the diving off-season they worked upriver in *champas* (seasonal agricultural and hunting camps), which they rebuild yearly. The fact that men participated in both migrant wage and migrant subsistence activities created a high rate of male absenteeism. Many social scientists contend that female-headed households and matrifocality thrive when men are absent from the household for long periods of time (Brettell 1986; Brogger and Gilmore 1997; Cole 1991; Gonzalez 1969, 1970; Helms 1971; Mohammed 1986; Rasmussen 1996; P. Scott 1995).

SERIAL MONOGAMY

Of thirty-two mothers in Kuri, thirteen claimed to have had children from only one man; twelve, from two to three spouses; and seven, from four to five spouses. The numbers are conservative because women often lied during interviews to hide the fact that some of their children were produced from outside or illicit unions. Also, most of the women who claimed to have had only one spouse were young and just beginning to have relationships with men. By the time a woman in Kuri approached the end of her reproductive years (around forty), she generally had had a series of semi-monogamous relationships that had produced children. Men generally had more spouses over their lifetime than the women, but the men's unions were harder to verify because their children were not all in the village (L. Herlihy 2006:48–49, 2007:139).

Gloria Wekker (2006) reports that low male salience in Surinam has to do with unstable unions (weak marriages) between husbands and wives. Because Afro-descendant Creole women have multiple and temporary unions, Wekker contends, a woman's lover is not tied to the household on a permanent basis, nor is he necessarily the father of her children.[5] H. B. K. Cook (1992:156) also recognizes that men in the husband-father role have little control over their wife's relatives who are not their biological children (see also Stack 1974; Fonseca 2001).

EMIGRATION AND EXOGAMY

I interviewed thirty-eight women to find out where the fathers of their children were from, before they came to Kuri (table 8). Most Kuri women (60 percent) practice a regional exogamy—they marry men from outside of the north coast villages. Miskitu men emigrate to the coast to find work as lobster divers and live with local women while they are employed. In the end these men return to their families and communities upriver or in other regions, leaving behind their coastal wives and children. Both Cook (1992) and Jan Brogger and David Gilmore (1997) contend that matrifocality typically occurs when men are outsiders who emigrate for work and then experience seasonal unemployment. This holds true for male lobster divers in Kuri.

TABLE 8. Kuri women's level of exogamy

Had children with someone from the village	3
Had children with someone from within the Río Plátano Biosphere Reserve	24
Had children with someone from outside the Río Plátano Biosphere Reserve	38

Source: L. Herlihy 2007:141

Verses of a Miskitu song performed by Wilintin Suarez and Eusebio Guevara additionally demonstrate that men come from far away to marry women along the coast, often returning to their homes after the marriage falls apart. The song tells of a common situation in Kuri, when women have sexual liaisons with other men while their husbands or boyfriends are at sea. As such, marriages in Kuri remain unstable.

Sirpi luhpi mairin	**Little-bitty woman**
Sirpi luhpi mairin	Little-bitty woman
man kumi dukiamra	just for you
tasbayamra balri	I came to your land
awal tara bilara	in the middle of a big river
kaubi na balri	I left paddling
sirpi luhpi mairin	little-bitty woman
kao tara mairin	the most important woman
kao sirpi mairin	the smallest woman
sirpi luhpi mairin	little-bitty woman
nahki na balras?	how could I not come?
sirpi luhpia mairin	little-bitty woman
man pali dukiamra	only for you
tasbayam ra balri	I came to your land
mai pliki wari, kuna	I came to get you, but
saura man ai munram	you only did bad things to me
saura pali ai munram	you did me wrong
saura pali ai munram	you did me wrong

SOCIAL ECONOMIES OF POWER

sirpi luhpi mairin	little-bitty woman
kao tara mairin	the most important woman
kao sirpi mairin	the smallest woman
sirpi luhpi mairin	little-bitty woman
kli tauwi auni	and so I went back again
Bilwira tauwi balri	I went back to Bilwi
sirpi luhpi mairin	little-bitty woman

CONFLICT AND DIVORCE

Marriages in Kuri are mainly sanctioned by local common law, in which couples that live together call each other *maia* (spouse). This kinship term is put into use frequently during courtship, as soon as the man moves into the woman's

FIGURE 24.
A wedding, Kuri
(PHOTO CREDIT:
Laura Herlihy)

house. Divorce is common and marked by the man moving out and dropping the term "maia" for his spouse. Locals distinguish among different types of marriages, including church, legal, and common-law marriages. The highest social status is accorded to those who had both church and legal marriages. Some of the wealthiest families arranged for the church reverends to marry a couple at home, followed by a wedding celebration.

Divorce is practiced not only by the young and immature. Two kukas threw their husbands out of the house during my stay in Kuri. The high rate of divorce and desertion in Kuri also adds to the absence of men in the community.

THE DOUBLE SEXUAL STANDARD

Kuri men are expected to keep outside lovers, but women are looked down upon for the same behavior. This double sexual standard operates along the north coast, igniting most interpersonal conflicts between women and men. Men joke among themselves about having outside girlfriends and openly sing songs that celebrate men's outside romances. The following song (performed by Wilintin Suarez and Eusebio Guevara) makes light of a married man having an extramarital affair. It explains how a man might find his girlfriend more appealing than his wife.

Maritkam Wihki lilam wal	Your wife or your lover
Maritkam wihki lilam wal	Your wife or your lover
ani want?	which one do you want?
lili want lili want lili want lili want	I want my lover
maritkam mairka kirbisi balram	when you come home to your wife
waikna almuk saura	ugly old man (she says)
ani wina aulma	where are you coming from?
pakitkam klauhwan	your pocket has holes
taki was, taki was, taki was	get out, get out, get out
ai mina pata ai lalka mata	and she kicks you in the head
taki was, taki was, taki was	get out of here, get out, get out
maritkam wihki lilam wal	your wife or your lover
ani want?	which one do you want?
lili want lili want lili want lili want	I want my lover

maritkam mairka kirbisi balram
dikiam wina aulma?
waikna almuk saura
mawan pali man lawan man
tat baku aras baku
biruku baku !alakai!

when you come home to your wife
where the heck have you been?
ugly old man
with her face all mad
like a piece of wood, like a horse
like a camel. Oh yeah!

maritkam wihki liliam want
ani want?
Lili want, lili want, lili want

your wife or your lover
which do you want?
I want my lover, I want my lover

maritkam mairka kirbisi balram
dikiam wina aulma
waikna almuk saura
taya bisbaya taki was
pakitkam klauhan
taki was
ai mina pata, ai lal pata
taki was, taki was, taki was

when you come home your wife (says)
where the hell have you been?
ugly old man
you stink, get out of here
you got a hole in your pocket
get out of here
she kicks you in the head
get out! get out! get out!

maritkam wihki lilam wal
ani want?
lili want, lili want, lili want

your wife or your lover
which one do you want?
I want my lover

lili lika kirbisi balri
dahlinki waikna
ani wina aulma
nara bal confitkam bris
kahlilka mahbra pisi
sikaritkam luhpia dis
amorki waikna
nara bal !ay!
ani wina aulma
daikiki susu
watata baku, srikoko baku
ay nara bal!

when you come home your lover
(says) my darling man
where are you coming from?
come here and eat your candy
after you eat your egg
smoke your little cigarette
my lover man
come here, oh!
where are you coming from?
undressing naked
like a little animal (she says)
oh, come over here!

maritkam wihki lilam wal	your wife or your lover
ani want?	which one do you want?
lili want lili want lili want lili want	I want my lover
lili lika kirbisi balri	coming home to your lover
nara bal dahlinki waikna	come here darling man
nara bal, dahlinki, nara bal	come here darling come here
ani wina aulma	where are you coming from
nara bal, damdamki	come here, my little sweet
maritkam wihki lilam wal	your wife or your lover
ani want?	which one do you want?
lili want lili want lili want lili want	I want my lover
upla kum watlara plapi sin wari	I ran to your house with the others
chicharron luhpia kiski na muni	you were making fried pig's skin
aikan taim	when you gave me a piece,
binka kaikri naipa palira	the noise left my teeth
tarrump tarrump tarrump	*chomp, chomp, chomp*
maritkam wihki lilam wal	your wife or your lover
ani want?	which do you want?
lili want lili want lili want	I want my girlfriend
lili latkara plapi na wari	I went to meet my girlfriend outside
aras luhpia na kumi na sakri	I found a little horse
amorki waikna ulsi uli na muni	come get on the horse my love
alki na walri nina palira	riding away, I heard behind me
paca paca pac paca paca pac	*clippity clop, clippity clop*
maritkam wihki lilam wal	your wife or your lover
ani want?	which one do you want?
lili want lili want lili want lili want	I want my lover

Men routinely complain that their wives are *uba waikna laik* (boy crazy). Comparatively, Kuri women say that their husbands are *uba wanina* (really jealous). "Uba waikna laik" and "uba wanina" are common cries in the battle of the sexes, a classic "he said, she said" argument that remains unresolved and is

SOCIAL ECONOMIES OF POWER

often the reason for a couple's divorce or separation. Women claim not to care if their husband have outside flings, commenting, "He's a man, isn't he? He's supposed to have other women." When women take sexual liberties similar to the men, however, Kuri men claim that these women are not feminine, act like men, or are *urkira* (whores).[6]

Matrilineal Trends

Low male salience thrives in Kuri households, which causes Kuri children to interact overwhelmingly with their mother's relatives. P. Scott (1995), studying urban Afro-Brazilians, identifies an emphasis on matrilineal kin as a defining characteristic of matrifocality. He defines matrifocality as "a complex web of relations constructed around the domestic group in which, even with the presence of a man in the house, the woman's side of the group is favored. This is evidenced in mother-child relations being more solidary than father-child relations, in the choice of residence, in the identification of known relatives, in exchange of goods and services, in visiting patterns and so on. All are stronger on the female side" (P. Scott 1995:287).

Following this definition, I examine an emphasis on matrilineal kin as a feature of Kuri matrifocality. In order to demonstrate the trend toward matrilineality in Kuri, I present and compare kinship data from the communities of Asang and Kuri. Most present-day information on Miskitu kinship has been provided by Helms in Asang. Helms (1971) documents Miskitu patrilocal residential patterns combined with a patrilineal system of kinship and decent. In Asang the nuclear family household (headed by a male in the husband-father role) tied into the larger kiamp, or patrilineal descent group, which included all members related through the male line. Fathers, brothers, and sons lived near each other throughout their lives. With patrilocality and patrilineality coexisting, all men and children of the patrilocal group were members of the same kiamp, symbolized by a common male surname. Helms describes how the kinship term *kiampka*, used with a male surname, such as Ferrera kiampka, referred to all members of the patrilineal descent group and to the area of the village where the family lived: "Asang can be identified as groups of people related to each other through kinship. In this sense the village loses a common unity and is seen instead as composed of many *kiampkas*—kinship groups to which an individual belongs by virtue of having the same family name. Because of the pattern of marital residence, the *kiampkas* tend to occupy separate geographical locations within the village" (Helms 1971:54–55).

At the time of Helms's study in the late 1960s, Asang residents conceptualized the village as being made up of twenty-seven kiamp with separate geographical locations (1971:55, 74). Helms shows on a map of the village that the Sanders, Joseph, and Bobb kiamp occupied the largest family grounds, although she states that the kiamp did not hold property. García's (1996b:13–23) later study of Asang finds that the male surname shared by a father and his descendants continued to define the kiamp. But she reports that sisters of the matrigroup, who commonly shared the male surname, upheld ties of the kiamp. García's conclusions differ from Helms's because García found Asang to have matrilocally organized patrilineal groups. What follows is a comparison and contrast of social organization between coastal Kuri and riverine Asang, based on research by Helms, García, and myself (table 9).

TABLE 9. Kuri and Asang: Household composition (%)

	COASTAL KURI		RIVERINE ASANG	
	1991	1997	1969	1993
Single nuclear family	32	16	54	50
Any combination with nuclear family	55	36	86	90
Female-headed household[a]	36	40	4	10
Half siblings in household	23	39	1	—
Adopted child of mother, daughter, or sister in household	32	36	2	—

Source: L. Herlihy 2007:144; Helms 1971; García 1996a
[a]Figures for Kuri include only households headed by single mothers, with no man whatsoever in the husband-father role.

In the larger community of Asang twenty-seven kiamps—symbolized by male surnames—occupied separate geographic territories. In Kuri the landscape could be divided into five neighborhoods, each dominated by a matrigroup. Each matrigroup is called by a kuka's name, such as "Lyvian kiampka," and cannot be identified by a male surname.

Loss of the Kiamp

Kuri residential groups are composed of many different kiamps, demonstrated by the presence of many different surnames in the matrilocal group. The Miskitu women pass down the father's surname to their offspring, whether married to the child's father or not. The combination of serial monogamy and patrinomy creates families in which brothers and sisters often have different last names—they are half siblings. As a result, Kuka Denecela's matrigroup (composed of five households) had thirty-five individuals with twenty different surnames in 1998 (table 10). Thus the kiamp, as described by Helms and even García, has diminished or possibly never existed in Kuri.

TABLE 10. Number of surnames per household in Kuka Denecela's matrigroup

	1991	1998
Kuka Denecela's household	4	4
Delfina's household	5	5
Ilabia's household	2	2
Enemecia's household	3	3
Tomasa's household	4	6
Total surnames	18	20

Source: L. Herlihy 2007:144–45

Weak ties often exist between members of a patrilineal descent group. Many men who emigrated to the coast to work and married locally eventually returned home, thus deserting their wives. In these cases, children were raised almost entirely by the mother's side of the family and rarely knew their father's relatives. In other scenarios, members of the same kiamp on the coast can be in conflictive relationships—if a man has or has had different wives along the coast, his children from these women can all have the same surname. Yet these relationships are filled with jealousies and rivalries, fueled by would-be co-wives. These families (technically of the same kiamp) do not share resources and try to avoid each other, often attending different churches. More and more, locals also use the term "kiamp" to refer to a matrigroup, such as "Lyvian kiampka"—a landowning residential kin group who trace their descent through the female line.[7]

For the coastal Miskitu the traditional kiamp, or patrilineal descent group, no longer functions to create society's most important social and economic ties. Instead, ties among members of the matrigroup have replaced those of the kiamp. Matrilineal descent seemingly thrives beneath a thin veil of patrimony, in which children inherit their father's surname. My analysis suggests that Kuri is characterized not only by matrilocality and matrifocality but also by increasingly matrilineal descent practices. Women's power in this society, then, in many ways has increased during the recent boom in the international (United States-Honduras) lobster economy.[8]

CHAPTER FOUR

Staying Afloat

Economics of the Matrigroup

This chapter demonstrates the economic ties that bind the women in Kuka Denecela's matrigroup. This matrigroup traditionally has survived through acts of reciprocity between family members on the coast and those who reside upriver in champas (family agricultural fields). Today subsistence agriculture has declined and Plátano Miskitu households mainly survive off of money provided by male lobster divers. Additionally, reciprocity between related families has decreased and some minor differences in social class have developed—the households with the most access to the divers' funds have the highest standard of living. Despite these changes, mothers, daughters, and sisters continue to make up the most important sharing network in coastal communities.

Most men now work in subsistence labors only during the lobster-diving off-season. The Honduran government enforces an annual moratorium, or veda, on lobster diving from mid-April through mid-August, when the lobsters breed. The moratorium occurs at a fortuitous time during the yearly agricultural cycle, when the locals burn and replant their fields. In Plátano Miskitu agricultural and hunting lands upriver, men employ slash and burn agriculture to produce crops like yucca, sugar cane, bananas, and more recently, rice and beans. The men typically do the more physically demanding clearing of the fields, but the women and children help with planting and harvesting activities.

Dodds (1998:13) states, "One successful 12-day outing can provide as much cash income to a diver as a year of working diligently in the fields to produce and market a cash crop." As a result, subsistence agricultural labor and hunting have greatly decreased, and families purchase most of their daily food from stores. These economic changes have put increasing pressures on men to risk their lives to bring up the elusive lobster, which mean more money for their families to spend in local stores. While the men are offshore diving in a deadly and dangerous occupation, the women left behind must fend for their families' economic survival. Related women bond together in matrigroups in which they raise children, share food, and invent strategies to gain access to the men's cash resources.

Kuka Denecela's Matrigroup

In 1998 Kuka Denecela's matrigroup included her households and those of her daughters, Enemecia, Tomasa, Ilabia, and Delfina; monthly income levels ranged from 600 to 3,500 lempiras within the matrigroup. Tomasa's and Ilabia's income placed them barely at survival level, while Kuka and Enemecia were even more economically disadvantaged. Most Kuri households (usually around seven people) need about U.S. $150 (2,070 lempiras) to survive each month.

Table 44. Monthly household income in Kuka Denecela's matrigroup (August–March 1998)

	LEMPIRAS	U.S. DOLLARS
Delfina's household	3,500	254
Tomasa's household	1,500	109
Ilabia's household	1,000	72
Enemecia's household	800	58
Kuka Denecela's household	600	43

Delfina, Kuka's oldest and wealthiest daughter, makes about $350 per month. She is married to elementary schoolteacher Siksto George, one of the few professionals in the region. Delfina's husband has a steady salary that is deposited in their Tegucigalpa bank account. She used his cash base to start a restaurant, bodega, and *trucha* (small store) in Kuri. Her son's cayuco (round-bottom canoe) with a motor makes it possible for her to pick up merchandise for her store via the Margarita cargo boat offshore. The cayuco and motor are also used in the family's ecotourism business, bringing one or two tour groups upriver each month (some through a tourist agency in La Ceiba). Delfina now also has a *hospedaje*, or tourist house, where visitors and ecotourists can reside. Her household of ten people includes her husband and son, a cook and her two children, and four other adopted children of female relatives.

Tomasa is Kuka's second-oldest and second most economically successful daughter. Tomasa's household earns $150 per month. She is a single mother who supports nine children. She has a bodega (a shack with a sometimes work-ing, gas-operated cooler) where she sells beer to divers. Delfina fronts her cases of beer to sell for a profit.

Ilabia is Kuka's youngest daughter, who was raised partially by Delfina. Ilabia's household exists at survival level, earning $100 per month. She is married with only two children living permanently in her household (two others live with Delfina). She has access to buzo money, with her husband being a cayuquero.

Kuka Denecela's household includes her husband, Octavio, two adopted children of her deceased daughter, and two great-grandchildren. Kuka's house-hold earns about $60 per month. She lives with Enemecia in Kuri and shares agricultural fields upriver in Liwa Raya. They have less access to cash than other women in the matrigroup because neither has a buzo as a permanent house-hold member. Because Enemecia and Kuka have such low household incomes, they cannot survive living only on the coast. They must also live off the land in Liwa Raya.

Enemecia, Kuka's middle daughter, is the closest to her mother and lives with her in a combined household. Enemecia's household earns $80 per month. She is a single mother with eight children in her household. Enemecia provides her children with vegetables, grains, meat, and fish in a respectable way in Liwa Raya. She even began to hunt with her father. Like her mother, Kuka Denecela, she thought it was disgraceful to earn money selling beer to lobster divers, as her sisters did on the coast.

Compared to other matrigroups, Kuka Denecela's has little access to sustained buzo salaries, with only one resident cayuquero, in Ilabia's home. Although not always permanent residents, sons, brothers, and nephews regu-larly donate money to the women in the matrigroup. Additionally, most of the sisters' households find ways to gain access to buzo money through the informal economy that revolves around the lobster-diving industry. Sisters in Kuka Denecela's matrigroup sell beer, rum, cigarettes, and marijuana to the men. This case study of Kuka Denecela's matrigroup shows how households adapt in diverse ways to the cash-oriented economics of coastal life. Three of five households in Kuka Denecela's matrigroup operate on money provided by buzos. The two women who sell goods to the buzos (Delfina and Tomasa) make the most money, followed by one woman who is married to a buzo (Ilabia), and then by two women with no access to buzo money (Kuka Denecela and Enemecia). These differences in income stratify the residential group, causing minor differences to occur in social class between sisters.

The families of Ilabia, Kuka Denecela, and Enemecia eat basic menu items of *wabul*, (mashed plantains and coconut water or milk), rice, beans, yucca, and fried plantains three times a day; some meals may have fish, crab, tortillas, and coffee. Meals of the wealthier sisters' families, Delfina's and Tomasa's,

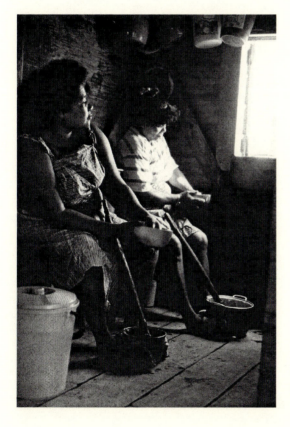

FIGURE 25.
Ilabia making wabul,
looking out a window
(PHOTO CREDIT:
Laura Herlihy)

include meat, eggs, milk, baked bread, spaghetti, tomato sauce, sardines, and instant soups. Delfina's household, with ten members, is the only one in the matrigroup that earns more than it spends and also has family savings; the other women live from day to day, trying to make ends meet. All of the sisters said that Delfina was rich, *lalah brisa* (literally, she has money), and that she upset the normal economy based on sharing between sisters. Yet the sisters continue to pool their funds to help a relative pay a fine or a healer or to finance a relative's trip to a hospital. To the extent possible, Kuka Denecela's matrigroup also incorporates more modern resources into their reciprocity networks. For example, Delfina fronts cases of rum and beer and cartons of cigarettes to her sister Tomasa to resell to the divers.

Cargo boats like the Margarita service Kuri and the north coast villages, bringing goods to permanent stores and to families with outboard motors, which locals attach to their cayucos. Cargo boats deliver wood for building houses, gasoline, Coca-Cola, beer, and smaller items like cookies that Kuri residents will resell from their homes. Delfina's son, Rollins, also called Plaisni (literally, youngest child), utilizes his motorized cayuco to meet the Margarita and bring the preordered and partially prepaid goods back to shore. Women

FIGURE 26. Delfina and Siksto receiving cargo from the Margarita boat (PHOTO CREDIT: Laura Herlihy)

and children of the matrigroup wait on the beach to unload cases of beer and carry them on their heads to Delfina's trucha.

Delfina's bodega is located in a separate structure, where beer is kept cool in a gas-powered refrigerator. She keeps ten cases for every three she sends to Tomasa's bodega, which is really just the patio that surrounds Tomasa's home. Named Aqui Me Queda Latara, (Here I wait outside), Tomasa's bodega serves room-temperature beer but is extremely popular with the local young men, or wahma, who flirt (triswaia) with the four or five tiara, or teenage girls, living there. Divers spend their money at Delfina's and Tomasa's bodegas, ending up drunk and penniless. Kuka did not like her daughters selling beer to the lobster divers but said they have no choice, "Como somos pobres."

Meat and Reciprocity

Men rarely hunt forest animals, having once provided meat such as spider monkeys, deer, tepesquintle (a type of nutria), and tapirs to the women, all of which are increasingly scarce today. Meat is mostly purchased with cash in coastal stores or in spontaneous markets established near a butchering site. A butchered cow will produce between U.S. $150 and $300 for the owner. Locals use their cattle like a savings account, killing a cow to finance a specific endeavor.

Many women complain about the loss of the important cultural practice of sharing meat. One mother in Kuri told me, "Before, whoever had the biggest piece of meat shared." She remembered the days when a neighbor returning from a successful hunt upriver would exchange a portion of meat for a big bunch of plátanos, or bananas. Nowadays, Kuka Gladys of Kuri said, "You just hear the people are in their house, but nothing comes." Even though sharing of subsistence items and forest game among friends has decreased, some sharing still occurs within matrigroups. When an animal is killed upriver or when a cow or pig is butchered for sale on the coast, the owners send game meat to their closest female relatives and sell the rest. Kuri women who own their own plots of plantains, yucca, or other crops upriver also continue to send allotments of their produce to their sisters and mother, and then they sell the rest to friends.

Prestige is bestowed on those with meat, and its local availability and price serve as important information to be shared among sisters. Meat is the resource that women of the matrigroup most desire from the wealthiest sister, Delfina. Delfina showcased her power when her sisters and mother had not eaten meat in weeks, denying them even small amounts. The sisters gossiped about

FIGURE 27. Delfina with meat (PHOTO CREDIT: Laura Herlihy)

Delfina, calling her *huba min* (stingy) and saying that when you visit her kitchen, "she keeps the lids on her pots." One day I witnessed Delfina lying to her own adopted daughter (really, her little sister) Ilabia, whom she looked in the eye and said, "Huina apu" (There's no meat). All the while Ilabia could smell the meat cooking and see it on Delfina's son's plate. Delfina undoubtedly acted this way because she knew that her sisters were poorer than she and less able to recipro-cate a gift of meat. I began to realize that both raw meat (*upan*) and cooked meat (*huina*) were scarce and prestigious commodities in the Kuri women's world of beans and rice (see also Nietschmann 1973). Once I cued into this, it seemed that meat was the main topic of every conversation. The women wanted to know who killed what, where, and when and how much it cost per pound.

Upriver there are no stores, and family members traditionally have farmed and hunted for a living and exchanged resources such as wild game and pro-duce for store-bought supplies from the coast. With no permanent stores

SOCIAL ECONOMIES OF POWER

upriver, family members depend on their coastal siblings for the purchased items that they need to survive. The relatively high cost of living on the coast has affected traditional sharing behaviors—it is more difficult to share or give away relatively costly, store-bought goods.

This causes emotional conflict, as Miskitu children are socialized to share and being stingy (*slabla*) is looked down on. On the north coast of the Plátano biosphere children and grown-ups alike regularly call out from afar, "Kum aik" (Give me one). Other times one hears a guilt-ridden voice saying, "Diera aikras" (You give me nothing). People are considered *kupia saura* (mean) if they do not share with friends or relatives, as was also noted by Helms (1971) among the Río Coco Miskitu people. Because of the social pressure to share what you have with others, some more easily swayed individuals gave away much of what they bought at stores, arriving at their homes with diminished amounts. More savvy Miskitu women returning from the store kept their newly purchased goods hidden in backpacks and pockets or under turbans (worn by grandmothers) to ensure that their goods made it home intact.

Cash-Oriented Obsessions

Nearly a hundred stores and bodegas now inundate the Plátano biosphere's seven-kilometer coastal byway between Ibans and Barra Plátano, an area that still does not have running water or electricity. Stores display an array of items on their shelves—clothes, rubber boots and sandals, medicines, flashlights, candles, matches, cigarettes, tobacco leaves, batteries, kerosene, brooms, large plastic tubs for washing clothes, smaller buckets and containers, machetes, knives, hammers, nails, pots and pans, notebooks, pens and pencils, inexpensive jewelry, perfumes, hair accessories, shampoo, toothpaste, soap, toilet paper, detergent and bleach, as well as foodstuffs such as coffee, flour, sugar, baking soda, yeast, salt, pepper, lard (*manteca*), canned sardines, spaghetti, instant soup, chips and other snacks, hard candy, powdered milk, oatmeal, cereal, and cookies. Some larger stores have gas-powered refrigerators to keep Kool-Aid, soda, and beer cold. Other foodstuffs, such as rice and beans grown locally, are kept in bulk; fresh-baked bread and, more infrequently, a few vegetables are displayed on the counter.

Customers gaze longingly at these goods and patiently wait at the counter to be attended by the owner. Even families that plant rice and beans upriver sell much of what they harvest to merchandise boats and other merchants. They

Figure 28. A store, Tasbapauni
(PHOTO CREDIT: Laura Herlihy)

then use this cash to buy small amounts of rice and beans daily from coastal stores at an inflated rate.

The stores along the Plátano biosphere's north coast mainly receive their goods from three merchandise boats, which arrive from La Ceiba every fifteen days during the lobster-diving season (August through March). When the merchandise arrives, women and children gather at stores and a market atmosphere prevails. Many women come to witness their neighbors' purchases, studiously observing who is buying what and for whom. This news will be passed around like gossip, as purchases reflect the current state of social relationships, especially between he who buys and she who receives.

During the diving season, when money is available, mothers visit stores and send their children daily to buy food and household items. Less frequently, women buy more luxurious items, such as clothes and toiletries. On special occasions they travel to larger stores to purchase items such as bicycles, mattresses, and jam boxes. Coastal villagers rely on sundry store-bought goods that cost twice as much as what one pays in bigger Honduran cities. The high cost of transporting merchandise to the remote region and price gauging by Ladino merchants are blamed for these elevated prices. Yet women continue to send

SOCIAL ECONOMIES OF POWER

their children to the store two or three times a day, figuring their finances from one meal to the next.[1]

Plátano Miskitu women in Kuri earn small amounts of cash selling produce, fruit, plants, medicines, and bread, and some of the younger women work for wages in the fields and shops or as domestics, keeping house, cooking, and washing and ironing clothes for the wealthier families. Women's earnings from these jobs, however, cannot cover the high cost of store-bought food to feed their families. Household survival depends on money and gifts provided by the buzos. While not every household in Kuri had access to buzo money, some had more than two divers under one roof. The Kuri women found multiple ways to access men's funds. Most local store owners give credit to the wives of responsible and successful divers. While a diver is offshore, the store owner allows the diver's wife to have an open charge account, to be paid when her husband returns to shore. The reputation of the diver usually determines the amount of credit given to the wife. This functions as a system of debt peonage, especially in the case of a few store owners who also own a lobster boat. Divers also give money to women in a form of gifts (*prisants*) or presents.[2] Once the man offers the money to a woman, the cash passes into the no-man's-land of her disposable household income, and it is considered unmanly for a man to recommend or ask how a woman might spend the money.

Several women with no husband-father present to help them clear their fields and no money to pay a hired worker did not plant at all during the years that I lived in Kuri. These economically challenged women lived off of what cash they could acquire in gifts from their boyfriends, sons, and brothers in the diving industry. Chapter 6 will describe the purely sexual and supernatural strategies that Plátano Miskitu women use to survive in the expanding market economy. Below are the more everyday strategies that a coalition of women used to garner cash and store-bought items from the male lobster divers.

Just Between Sisters

Lying (Kunin Aisaia)

Women told me repeatedly that a good sister protects her sister by lying. For example, when a diver returned home he expected his wife to be waiting for him with a clean house and a hot meal. Yet there were times when boats returned without warning or in the middle of the night. In these situations a wife may not be prepared for her husband's arrival. If a buzo wife was not at home, sisters would lie to their sister's husband about her whereabouts and then run to warn her that her husband was at home.

Women at times also lied about money. Mindel had left one hundred lempiras in his home to buy nails for the house, which were due to arrive during his absence. While Mindel was off at sea, Ilabia went through the cash a little bit each day, spending it on raffle numbers, soda, beer, and cigarettes. On the eve of Mindel's impending arrival, Delfina, the oldest sister and alpha female, called a meeting and instructed the sisters to lie in unison. What the coalition would tell Mindel was that his youngest child (the one who could not yet talk) had gotten sick and needed an injection on the llano (the flatlands on the way to Belén). No one wanted Ilabia to be punished with a beating.

Kuri women had a reputation for lying, probably because they were a tight-knit group. Accordingly, their boyfriends feared being tricked and imagined the worst. Men told me that some local women acted like good wives when their boyfriend-diver was onshore but took on lovers the minute the diver headed out to sea. Perhaps even worse than having your girlfriend or wife cheat on you, they explained, was having her spend money on a boyfriend (married woman commonly gave gifts to younger men). A lonely man at sea hated to think of his hard-earned money going toward feeding his wife's lover.

Tagalong

Kuri women purposefully searched out only paid divers. Intoxicated divers with money in their pockets were sitting pigeons or putty in the women's hands. The poorest women in Kuri, they told me, were infamous for robbing divers who passed out in their homes and going through their pants once they took them off. The absolute worst scenario for a lobster diver was waking up on the beach with empty pockets and a hangover, unable to remember who they had been with the night before. Inebriated divers also were known to drop money regularly. There was no electricity or lights, and on dark nights, divers commonly staggered and swayed, unable to hold still long enough to remain in a friend's flashlight focus. A stoned diver purchasing beer often missed his pocket opening and dropped money to the ground. Additionally, many divers had nerve damage in their muscular hands and gnarly fingers from being pinched by claws as they plucked lobsters from their beds. Given these factors, behind many divers are two groups, those trying to access his cash and those trying to guard it.

Women instructed their children to follow behind divers, hoping that they would stumble on some of their earnings. Women and children also followed behind intoxicated divers to protect them. Mothers remained on the levee and sent younger children to watch their son's back, just in case money dropped to the ground during a scuffle or purchase. Kuka Livian and her children all followed Apudu (Kuka Livian's son) to Two Man Discotheque. In fact, children lined the doors and windows of the disco and even peered through openings between the wooden slats of walls and floorboards, spying on their brothers, sons, and uncles. Divers typically bought rounds of six to ten beers for their friends, an occurrence that would be reported immediately to their older family members on the beach levee.

Bringing Home the Cookies
Miskitu women staged random encounters with divers. Within hours of a boat's return, some women would leave their homes with empty bags and head for the nearest store. Children would wait optimistically for their mothers to return and, running to greet them, they ask, "Dia ai bribalram" (What did you bring me?). Mothers would open their sacks like Halloween revelers and hand over the loot—galletas (cookies), frescos (sodas), and chorros (chips). The children would demolish the goods within minutes. The buzos had been generous that night.

Resale
Once I accompanied some sisters from a neighboring matrigroup to Two Man Disco. They had brought an empty bucket with them, which they quietly tucked under the table. The oldest sister, Rosali, told us, "Drink slowly and keep one open beer in front of you at all times." The entire time Rosali placed the beers the divers were buying for us in the bucket under the table. The divers, too blind to notice, continued buying us beer. We eventually collected two dozen or so beers in the bucket and, when the divers were not looking, we brought them all back to Kuri. After Two Man's beer was depleted (dahn or apu takan), the same divers who bought beer for us came to Kuri in search of more beer. Rosali sold the men the same beer that they had bought for us. This was pure profit.

Bait and Switch
On a night when dozens of lobster divers were on the prowl, Rosali told a group of divers that she was having a "party" at her bodega and that attractive young women would be there. She then invited the more desirable young women in Kuri to have a free drink that night. After the divers (not Rosali) bought drinks for the young women, the women departed for their homes, leaving the divers

high and dry. Playing on their disappointment, Rosali then arranged for other, less attractive, older women to sleep with the divers (perhaps women just passing through Kuri). She put a mattress on the floor in a nearby house whose owners were upriver, and one in her own house, sending the children to sleep at their aunts' houses—Rosali's children arriving sleepy-eyed with sheets and pillows in tow were a sure sign to others that Rosali was making money that night. On a good night—when she sold beer and other items, like rum, cigarettes, chorros, and maybe marijuana, and when she received a finder's fee for arranging for the men's housing and women—Rosali could make up to U.S. $80–$100. This occurred quite infrequently, maybe once or twice a diving season, when everything worked out just right.

The Pusher
Rosali and two of her sisters went out one night, their backpack filled with rum bottles. They headed east for Utla Almuk and asked Rosali's half-brother to spread the word that she had rum for sale on the beach. They hid behind beached canoes and *uva* (sea-grape) trees.

FIGURE 29. Sisters Tomasa and Enemecia
exchanging money (PHOTO CREDIT: Laura Herlihy)

After Rosali and her sisters got rid of three of the four large bottles of rum (at sixty lempiras apiece), they came out from behind the uva trees and entered a hut on the edge of Utla Almuk. Inside the beach hut music blared from a jam box. Only one candle burned in the dimly lit room. The sisters sat in plastic chairs and hid the backpack, now with just one bottle left inside. The owner would surely have kicked them out had he known the women were peddling liquor at prices cheaper than his own. Men and women inside the dimly lit hut talked in slurred, low voices, and a wasted diver spit on the ground repeatedly. Other male divers looked clandestinely for prostitutes, booze, marijuana, and even cocaine. One couple fell down dancing to ranchero music, but no one dared to pay attention. Anonymity ruled the night.

Rosali made her last sale of the night and the sisters left the hut and scampered home along the beach. Someone behind them signaled by shining a flashlight down at the ground. Already out of rum, Rosali flashed her light twice on the ground, indicating she was done. Proper flashlight behavior, known by all the locals, seems to be artfully perfected by those who sell contraband goods at night.[3]

My case study of a matrigroup in Kuri demonstrates that while sharing of subsistence items has decreased, cash resources (including meat) have been incorporated into reciprocity networks. Most significantly, male members redistribute their funds within the matrigroup in which they were raised—sharing their salaries with their girlfriends, sisters, aunts, and mother. In turn, women lend money to each other in various ways, especially by pooling their funds when a child is sick or when a family member must travel. Related women also front each other money to buy beer and other items, which are then sold to the divers. Sisters also manipulate the divers into giving them money and purchased goods using everyday tactics. Women of the matrigroup, then, are adapting to the market economy by incorporating modern resources into their reciprocity networks. This contrasts with the findings of Christopher Kimblad (2001, 2010), who describes two separate economies in the Miskitu community of Tasbapauni (Nicaragua)—the traditional one based on reciprocity and sharing and the newer, cash-oriented economy. He explains that cash resources are not commonly shared among community members. My research in Kuri suggests a different scenario, where cash is incorporated into the economy of the matrigroup based on sharing and reciprocity. The matrigroup remains the main socioeconomic network in coastal Miskitu communities. Therefore, contradictory gender and power relations exist in Kuri's matrifocal domestic groups, where men have access to wages through migrant labor yet women control social relationships and make household economic decisions (see also Menon 1995; Smith 1956, 1996). Indeed, Kuri is a town supported by men but administered by women.

CHAPTER FIVE

Into the Deep

The Lobster Diver

THE LOBSTER DIVER HAS BECOME THE PROTOTYPICAL MASCULINE identity, a macho-man who risks his life in a dangerous profession to provide money to his family. Lobster diving has reigned as the only profession available for men on the Miskito Coast since the 1970s. About 90 percent of the men in Kuri and in the larger coastal region were lobster divers. Lobster divers are paid per pound of lobster; skillful divers are more successful hunting and harvesting lobster. The most manly men are known for killing the most lobster and giving away the most money and gifts to the women. Miskitu masculinity, then, has become directly linked to a man's cash-earning potential. In fact, this chapter documents an almost complete mercantilization of Miskitu men's bodies.

THE LOBSTER-DIVING INDUSTRY

When I embarked on my doctoral field research in 1997, Honduras reaped an estimated U.S. $35 million from its export fisheries industry, much of which was based on lobster extraction. Seafood companies located in the Honduran Bay Islands, due north of the Miskito Coast, work with boat owners who hire

Figure 30.
A lobster diver (PHOTO
CREDIT: Laura Herlihy)

Miskitu men as lobster divers and younger men and boys as canoemen to hunt spiny lobster (*Panulirus argus*). Their catches are purchased and processed in eight major seafood plants in the Bay Islands. Most of the lobster is shipped to Florida, where U.S. restaurants like Red Lobster (part of Darden Restaurants, Inc.) and Sysco Foods purchase spiny lobster tails (Dodds 1998).

The lobster economy along the north coast employs nearly seven hundred indigenous Miskitu and other men as deepwater lobster divers, representing about one-fifth of the four thousand divers (buzos) and canoemen (cayuqueros) in the entire Honduran Moskitia (Herlihy and Herlihy 1991:10; Proyecto Nautilo 1993:6).[1] Miskitu men initially became known as deepwater divers for free diving, or diving without tanks. When the industry began in the 1970s, lobsters were plentiful and the divers hunted them in relatively shallow waters. The divers began using tanks about thirty years ago, which enables them to dive deeper and stay underwater longer. Divers increasingly must descend deeper and deeper to find lobsters, now an overexploited and diminished natural resource. Dodds (1998:89) reports that in 1992 Miskitu divers from the reserve's north coast made 10 lempiras (U.S. $1) per pound of lobster. By the 1998 season I witnessed the divers receiving between 35 and 40 lempiras (U.S. $2.53–$2.89) per pound.

SOCIAL ECONOMIES OF POWER

Twenty-five lobster boats, mainly from the Bay Islands, operated during the 1997–1998 season. Lobster divers contributed "an estimated U.S. $3.2 million per year into the economies of the Plátano reserve's north coast villages" (L. Herlihy 2005:37). From August to March boats owners pick up the Miskitu divers near the coastline and take them offshore to hunt spiny lobsters. Men work for ten to twelve days at a time, resting for a few days before shipping off again. Only the tails are taken from these relatively small, spiny lobsters, and divers receive their pay by the pound. The boat owners then drop the men off along the shore and take the lobster tails to the Bay Islands for packaging and shipping to the United States, eventually to be consumed in U.S. restaurants (Dodds 1998:87–88).

Buzos and cayuqueros may work a few trips or many or combine diving with their agricultural duties. Many combine occupations creatively—one buzo is also a part-time pastor for the Evangelical Pentecostal Church. Men generally earn more at the beginning of the season, when the lobster beds are full, and their earnings decrease as the season continues. The first trip of the diving season is, by far, the largest take of lobsters for the entire season. Even men who work as teachers and professionals may partake in the first trip of every season to reap this yearly benefit. In Kuri most men usually took two trips per month during the diving season.

All divers claim that their take-home pay depends largely on luck. Nevertheless, an experienced diver is generally more successful than a beginner. Most inexperienced buzos make around U.S. $150 on each trip, and the more experienced divers can earn twice as much. An average annual take for an experienced buzo in Kuri (taking two trips per month during the eight-month season) is about 66,240 lempiras (U.S. $4,800). Canoemen earn about 20 percent of what a diver makes (Dodds 1998:89). Estimating divers' incomes proves difficult, as they can have trips when they are extremely lucky, making up to 12,000 lempiras (U.S. $870), or unlucky trips when they earn nothing and come home empty-handed. Also, many divers get injured or become ill and miss part or all of a diving season. One buzo commented to me, "The good divers know that the real money is had by a diver who sees everything in the ocean as a resource and grabs everything he sees—conch, *mustro* [a type of fish], turtles [*aksbil*], fish, etc. He can end up selling it all in the islands when unloading the lobster. . . . The good divers were lucky [or had *suerte*], but even the good divers could come back with nothing. Anything was possible for one trip, especially if the *liwa(s)* [water spirits] were involved."

Coastal villagers may find employment related to the lobster industry other than being a buzo or cayuquero. Many men work on boats as captains, *marineros* (sailors), workers who fill the tanks with air or package and freeze the lobsters, boat mechanics, and cooks and their assistants (*plunki*). Onshore about two dozen people, mainly men, work as *sacabuzos* for boat captains, while both men and women work as *comanches* (assistants) to sacabuzos. Dodds (1998:91) calls sacabuzos "diver foremen" and notes that they are responsible for the boat having enough divers and canoemen to leave for sea. Sacabuzos also pay divers an advance before leaving, so that their families can buy food from the store while the men are at sea. Many divers count on large advances, receiving upwards of 800 lempiras (U.S. $58), while their canoemen receive a smaller sum. Once the diver is back on shore, a sacabuzo pays him based on the number of pounds of lobster he caught. Advances are subtracted from the diver's total earnings. In this way, divers and canoemen have spent much of their pay before they return to shore.

Boys to Men

Lobster diving is a gender-specific job that is blatantly exclusive of women. Heading out to sea is a teenage boy's first real separation from his matrigroup, and his first trip to sea functions as a coming-of-age ritual. Anthropologists applying post-Freudian analysis (Gilmore 1991; Gregor 1985; Murphy 1956) have pointed out that the separation from a female identity may be especially

Figure 3.1.
A boy chasing a man in a cayuco
(photo credit: Laura Herlihy)

dramatic for boys in matrifocal cultures. My own research found this to be true. A younger cayuquero begins by apprenticing for a diver who is an older male relative. A mother's brother or uncle (*tahti*) commonly takes on the role of male mentor to his sister's son (*tuban*). The tahti initiates the tuban by teaching him the tricks of the lobster trade and also how to behave while back onshore. After returning from sea the tahti often buys the young man his first alcoholic beverages and sexual experiences. A tuban-tahti (nephew-uncle) kinship relationship exists between most cayuqueros and their buzo partners. Yet these respectful kinship terms of reference are usually adopted regardless of the actual relationship between the canoeman and diver. Cayuqueros become lobster divers within a few years and begin mentoring their own younger nephews as canoemen.

Travel and Mobility

Men leave their riverine communities, traveling to the coast by canoe. They continue their treks offshore to fishing banks in the territorial waters of Colombia, Jamaica, Nicaragua, Cuba, and the Cayman Islands. Mariano, a twenty-something diver, originally paddled his way to Kuri from the community of Awas, on the middle Río Patuca. He often recounted his journey, once joking with me, "From the big river, I came paddling." This referred to a popular buzo song that he previously helped me to record.

Awal tara wina	**From the big river**
Awal tara wina kaubi na balri	I came from the big river paddling
wark lalka kumi doña Isa makikan	I found a boss named doña Isa
warki dukia na sakri	She found me work and I got ready
dwairka na saki muni	I got out my cayuco
kwahi na saki muni	I got my paddle out
surungki taki muni	and got my backpack ready
awal tara wina kaubi na balri	I came from the big river paddling
pas karma luri	I first passed
Brus karma makikan	the *barra* named Brus
las karma luri	the last barra I passed
Karataska karma makikan	was named Caratasca
awal tara wina kaubi na balri	I came from the big river paddling[2]

Boat captains illegally enter international waters to search for lobster. Several boats have been caught by authorities in illegal waters, causing boat captains to dock in distant lands. Captains are detained by the authorities while the divers are allowed to come ashore, returning to sleep in the boat. Once a boat from the coast was detained for a month in Jamaica, leaving unknowing families on the north coast. When the divers returned, the men had acquired distinctly Raastafarian influences in their vernacular speech and their clothing styles. More recently, when boats were detained, Miskitu divers adopted newer, gangster-style popular culture and dialect, which spreads out from Miami through the Caribbean. Traversing distant lands and waters brings prestige to men, who return with foreign goods and new life experiences (see also Helms 1993). North coast residents consider these divers to be peripatetic and chic. Part of Miskitu manhood is retaining one's mobility and ability to leave home at a moment's notice.

Danger and Death

Achieving full Miskitu manhood requires men to participate in a dangerous occupation (see also Gilmore 1991). Nearly 15 percent of all lobster divers in the Río Plátano Biosphere Reserve (over a hundred men) have been injured, paralyzed, or killed while lobster diving. The boats have no decompression chambers on board, and boat owners and captains do not provide proper training or safe equipment to the divers. They are forced to use old diving equipment without depth gauges (Meltzoff and Schull 1999; World Bank 1999). The divers also use cocaine and marijuana on boats, often before they dive, descending to dangerous depths, and they take more than triple the recommended number of dives per day.[3]

The most serious health problem that divers develop related to their work is the bends, also called caisson disease and decompression sickness, a sometimes fatal disorder marked by neuralgic pain and paralysis, distress, and often a collapse in breathing that is caused by the release of gas bubbles (as of nitrogen) in body tissue.[4] This happens to divers who ascend too quickly from the depths of the ocean and experience a rapid decrease in air pressure after a stay in a compressed atmosphere. The locals refer to this affliction as liwa mairin, or Mermaid sickness (Barrett 1992; Dennis 2004; García 1996a; L. Herlihy 2005; Pérez Chiriboga 2002).

The Mermaid water spirit, according to local lore, is the creator and owner of all resources from the ocean, lagoons, or rivers, including fish, shrimp, turtle,

FIGURE 32.
Lobster
divers at
work, by
A. Bizmark

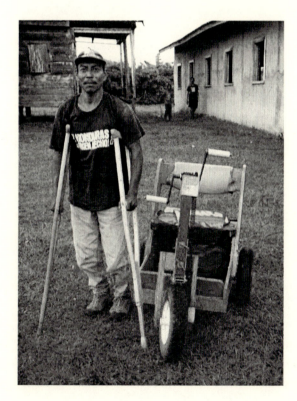

FIGURE 33.
An injured lobster
diver (PHOTO CREDIT:
Laura Herlihy)

and lobster; she punishes those who overexploit her resources with sickness and death. This belief acts as a check on greed within Miskitu society, revealing an autochthonous concept of natural resource conservation—a balance must be maintained between the human and natural world (see chapter 7 for more on the Mermaid).

The song below (performed by Wilintin Tejeda and Eusebio Guevara) describes the death of a diver. Wilintin and Eusebio sang from the perspective of a diver about to be lifted out of a life preserver and placed in a coffin for others to view at his wake (*velorio*). A fatalistic mentality prevails, and divers often ruminate about their own death in song. The last verse also reaffirms that many divers are from villages far from the coast, and they fear dying alone.

Yang saura na	**I'm here dying**
Yang saura na	I'm here dying
yang saura na, yang saura na	I'm dying here
twilp dais na alkikan	I reached twelve days
turki saura na brisatma	and I bring to you a sad story
preservka lana na bilara	I'm inside of the life preserver
mai kupi na lakan kan	my heart was turning over for you
yang Saura na	I'm dying now
yang Saura na	I'm dying now
ini oy	oh my
ini oy	oh my
yang saura na	I'm dying now
na wina apia	I'm not from here
lalma wina	I'm from the north
yang saura na	I'm dying now
muna wina	I'm from the west
yang saura na	I'm dying now

A diver's health is further at risk because of the poor living conditions on boats. Divers find it hard to sleep in their canoes (or in wooden bunks) with the blaring sound of the boat's motor and frequently rough seas that cause seasickness. More than a few boat captains are involved in the trafficking of cocaine between countries, also trading a portion of the lobsters for cocaine (Meltzoff and Schull 1999; Nietschmann 1997). Divers on cocaine-trafficking lobster boats can suffer violent deaths—one of Kuka Denecela's sons was gunned down at a lobster bank in Nicaragua. Some captains have abandoned divers and their canoemen when being chased by Coast Guard boats and helicopters. Two divers told me stories of how they followed stars at night to return to shore, catching rainwater in their shorts, which they wrung out in their mouth to fend off dehydration.

Problems additionally arise between divers on board having to do with witchcraft (*maña negra* or *waukataya*). Living in close quarters on small boats, at times with strangers from other villages, creates a climate of suspicion and distrust. Especially while ingesting drugs like cocaine, divers may become paranoid that others are using "black magic" to harm them. Many divers carry a *tup*, or amulet, usually made of an umbilical cord and plants, which can function as a charm to find lobsters, a counter to the witchcraft of others, or as protection from the Mermaid. Nicaraguan Miskitu men used similar amulets to protect themselves in battle during the Nicaraguan revolution (Pérez Chiriboga 2002).

Divers commonly report fights breaking out on boats because of stolen items, such as cassettes, amulets, or clothing. In preparation for trouble, many divers imbibe *aiklabaia saihka* (fighting medicine) to give them extra force and power when fist-fighting with another diver. Isabel Pérez Chiriboga (2002:222–28) found these practices among Nicaraguan Miskitu soldiers but called them "secretos." Other divers use *suapaihka saihka* (weakening medicine) to take away their enemy's strength. Due to potential flare-ups between divers, boat captains often bring marijuana onboard and encourage divers to smoke cigarettes to calm their nerves.

Many churches employ an empty air tank as an ersatz bell, which they strike with a steel rod to announce the beginning of service, an emergency, or the death of a community member. The slow striking of a diver's air tank, indicating death, reminded me of the John Donne quote, "Never send to know for whom the bell tolls; it tolls for thee." The constant threat of death to the divers causes many uncomfortable good-byes to children, wives, and mothers at the beach. Ariano regularly said to me upon departing, "It's been nice to know you, and I wanted to say good-bye in case I don't make it back." Many women embrace their kinsmen while praying out loud for a healthy homecoming. They watch the men and boys, most wearing backpacks, paddle out to sea in small dugout canoes. Their cayucos may turn over more than once from strong, breakwater waves crashing over the bow, but the buzos eventually make it to the boat, then head out to sea, fading from the shore's view.

FIGURE 34. A kuka watching her son leave on
a lobster boat (PHOTO CREDIT: Laura Herlihy)

All mothers would ideally want their husbands, sons, and brothers to dedicate themselves only to agricultural work. Yet there is little choice in an economy where families increasingly need cash but there are no other cash-earning
opportunities available. The women fear for the men's lives but say, "There's no
other hope, since we're poor" (Como somos pobres, no hay otra esperanza).
Kuka Denecela commented to me, "I don't want my sons to dive, but what can
we do, we need the money. . . . I already lost one son who died at the bank, and
I have two sons who are divers now. What will I do when they bury then in
the cemetery? I won't be able to talk to them. They won't be able to pass by my
house on Sundays."

The buzos also participate in a hazardous culture back onshore. Buzo
behaviors include drinking excessive amounts of alcohol and brawling. With
no financial institutions in the region, men carry around huge amounts of
cash (and sometimes cocaine) in their backpacks or pockets. Dark nights with
no electricity or lights sometimes brought a fearful and deadly atmosphere.
Suspicious strangers, perhaps men who immigrated to the coast for work, seem

SOCIAL ECONOMIES OF POWER

to lurk behind every coconut tree and beached cayuco. Many buzos carry pistols and knives to protect themselves from robbery or murder. These arms frequently are pulled out when arguing with others in a drunken stupor. Drinking and fighting are considered "manly" behaviors, which adds to the danger associated with buzo identity (see also Gilmore 1991).

THE BOOM AND BUST SELF

Lobster divers have unstable access to money. Even when the lobster-diving season is in full swing, Miskitu divers can get lucky or unlucky on any one trip, bringing in a huge amount of lobster or next to nothing. When men have lucky trips they call themselves "lalah dusa" (literally, money trees), taking pride in the fact that their money supports Miskitu families; when divers have unlucky trips, they use the words "lalah apu" (to be flat broke) to describe their sad and downtrodden emotional state.

The song below, "Lalah dusa" (Money tree), reveals that when the divers have money in their pockets, they arrogantly refer to themselves as *millionarios* (in Spanish). The songs mention that teenagers, children, and grandparents are happy when the buzos arrive, revealing that the men's funds support all sectors of the population. Lalah dusa is a funny expression, similar to the English "money bags," which also implies that the men are valued for one reason: their income. The song also shows the strong relationship between ethnic identity and occupation and the pride that Miskitu men have developed due to their international reputation as skilled divers.

Lalah dusa	Money tree
Yang nani sika yang nani	We are who we are
yang nani sika lalah dusa	we are the money trees
yang nani sika yang nani	we are who we are
yang nani sika lalah dusa	we are the money trees
kampani tara tilara	within a big company
wark tara dauki kan	having done important work
yang nani sika yang nani	we are who we are
kabu un purara iwisna	we live over the sea shore
yang nani sika yang nani	we are who we are
yang nani sika lalahka dawan	we are the money owners

butka tara dawanka	we rule the big fishing boats
baranka tara dawanka	we rule the great ravines
tawanka tara dawanka	we rule the big towns
Miskitu tara dawanka	we rule the great Miskitu people
yang nani sika yang nani	we are who we are
yang nani sika lalah dusa	we are the money trees
kampani butka nani ba	when the company's boats
kustara bribalan	brought them [the men] to the coast
dama nani lilia sa	the grandfathers are happy
kuka nani lilia sa	the grandmothers are happy
tiara nani lilia sa	the teenage girls are happy
lalah dusa aula taim	when the money trees arrive
tuktan nani lilia sa	the children are happy
almuk nani lilia sa	the elders are happy
lalah dusa aula taim	when the money trees arrive
kuka nani lilia sa	the grandmothers are happy
tiara nani lilia sa	the teenage girls are happy
tuktan nani lilia sa	the children are happy
lalah dusa na dukiara	because of the money trees

The next song, "Zero man zero" (Flat broke), demonstrates Miskitu men's self-identity during an economic bust situation. "Zero man zero" tells the story of a lobster diver who wants to buy clothes for his children and food for his wife and in-laws. The diver has worked at sea for twelve days, but when it comes time to figure out his pay, he realizes he has earned next to nothing. The diver sings apologetically to his in-laws—he can buy them only one pound of salt and one pound of sugar. In these personal bust situations, a Miskitu man's self-worth is low. Miskitu men act depressed when they do not earn the money that their family needs to survive.

Zero man zero	**Flat broke**
Zero man zero	Flat broke
daipnara audi wis	say hello to my father-in-law
sukurira audi wis	say hello to my mother-in-law
yang maka balauna	I'm going away [passing in front]

yang tuktan kwalka pliki	looking for my children's clothes
mairin kwalka pliki	looking for my wife's clothes
yang maka balauna	I'm getting ready to leave
kabura balauna	I'm going out to sea
doce dias ai alkan	when I finished twelve days
kli taui balri kan	I turned back for home
maka taimki daukri taim	when I figured out my earnings
zero man zero	zero man zero
daipnara audi wis	say hello to my father-in-law
sukurira audi wis	say hello to my mother-in-law
yang maka balauna	I'm going away
kabura balauna	I'm going out to sea
sal paun kum na bribia wis	tell them to buy a pound of sugar
sukar paun kum na bribia wis	tell them to buy a pound of salt
umpira sna na	I'm a poor man now
dia lika blikamni?	what can I send them?
umpira sna na	I'm a poor man now
dia lika blikamni?	what can I send them?
umpira sna na	I'm a poor man now
dia lika blikamni?	what can I send them?
Zero man zero	Flat broke
Zero man zero	Flat broke

The first song, "Lalah dusa," celebrates the Miskitu men's concept of self as a cash-earner in the lobster-diving economy—men feel like rock stars in their communities. The second song, "Zero man zero," laments the men's concept of self during an economic bust situation—men feel impotent and useless. The Miskitu divers, then, define themselves by two emotional states—"being with money" and "being without money." The songs illustrate the importance of earning cash to the self-worth and self-esteem of Miskitu men. When divers are lalah apu (broke), they complain that no woman would desire them. These findings also support Helms's (1971) theory of boom and bust behavioral patterns within the purchase society.

Those regarded as the most masculine members of society are divers who kill the most lobster, make the most money, and give the most away, particularly to women. These relatively rich, macho men are treated like heroes. Arriving on shore, they bring a bag of lobster tails, conch, and fish for their household to enjoy. After being paid back by the sacabuzo, they head to the local stores to buy beer and other merchandise. The divers draw crowds at stores, and many residents follow them there, hoping to receive a Coke or more. Some tagalongs may get angry and call the diver "slabla" (stingy) or "min" (mean) if they receive nothing. Perceived manhood, then, rests equally on one's lobster-hunting abilities and one's level of generosity. Early studies of economic anthropology by Franz Boas (1981), Bronislaw Malinowski (1984), and Marcel Mauss ([1922] 1990) first brought attention to the logic of prestige economies. Mauss's ([1922] 1990) *The Gift* describes how one's generosity in gift-giving reflects the prestige and status of the giver more than the receiver. These concepts relate to men's economic practices along the Miskito Coast.

FIGURE 35. Lobster divers vagando
(PHOTO CREDIT: Laura Herlihy)

Miskitu divers commonly spend their money celebrating in a ritualized activity known in Spanish as *vagando* (carousing together). Young men vagando exchange their wealth for social prestige within their own, divers' culture. These divers celebrate each safe and healthy return to shore by buying rounds of drinks (rum and beer), cigarettes, marijuana, and even cocaine for each other, and they give gifts of money to women, often after sexual liaisons. After two or three days of vagando and womanizing, many young divers end up with little or no money to bring home to their families. What little money does remain is given to their girlfriends, mother, and sisters. Karin Tice (1995), among the Kuna of Panama, reports a similar pattern of lobster divers spending their wages partying before they return home. Cecile Jackson (2001) interprets the added element of spending wages on alcohol and other luxury items and withholding winnings from the household as pathological. However, Rachel Adams and David Savran (2002) note that participating in male-bonding activities is an essential element to becoming a man across cultures (see also Chant 2001; Gilmore 1991; Herdt 1982). Accordingly, Miskitu men spend money vagando as part of their initiation into manhood, an early stage in the manhood puzzle. Young divers tend to blow most of their winnings partying, but older divers spend their money more wisely.

A Day in the Life of Alcero

Alcero, Kuka Denecela's plaisni (youngest child, or seca leche in Spanish) was a twenty-one-year-old lobster diver. He had returned to shore on a Friday and by Sunday was still vagando (roaming around and up to no good) with his friends. Alcero entered Kuka's house with a bottle of cheap Rum Plata in his hand. Kuka often lectured Alcero about the dangers of being a buzo, but she willingly accepted the money he gave her. Some buzos, Kuka explained, did not give any money to their mothers. She was grateful for the 300 lempiras he gave her after every trip and for the smaller amount of his advans (advance pay) that he gave her before he left for a trip. These were small amounts compared to what he spent drinking, carousing, and gifting his wife and other girlfriends. By the end of the day on Sunday, however, Alcero would be lalah apu (flat broke).

Kuka told Alcero, "Lie down and take a nap," but Alcero opened another bottle of Rum Plata. Kuka grabbed the bottle and snapped, "Put your head down and go to sleep."

Alcero closed his eyes, barely. Suddenly jumping up, he announced to his wife and mother, "I have to find a woman." He continued the drunken rave, "I'm going to Barra Plátano to find a woman."

Kuka responded, "You'll be lucky if you make it to Utla Almuk." She knew that Alcero could not make it far in his condition. As Alcero stumbled out of the house and joined his friends, Kuka stood in the door and yelled behind him, "How can you cross the Río Plátano half blind?"

Alcero did not return that night. Knowing she would be concerned, Kuka's cousin from the next village, Utla Almuk, came to her house at sunrise. She reported to Kuka that Alcero was asleep in her home. According to the woman, Alcero took one step in the door, fell flat on his face, and passed out for the night.

That afternoon Alcero resurfaced at Kuka's home. His pockets empty, he had a pounding headache. To make matters worse, a pesky sacabuzo (the diver foreman and headhunter) was trying to get him to leave for his boat, the Armak III. The sacabuzo was getting on his already thin nerves when Alcero left from the back of his mother's house, successfully escaping for another hour to drink beer with friends. When the sacabuzo finally tracked him down on the beach, Alcero punched him squarely on the chin, knocking him out, and then proceeded to get into his cayuco and head out to the nearest of two boats. Thoroughly intoxicated, he paddled toward the wrong boat, entertaining everyone on shore, who, amid laughter, yelled to him to paddle toward the other boat.

I ran into Alcero during his next homecoming celebration. A group of young divers were taking swigs from a bottle of rum, passing it among themselves. When the bottle emptied, Alcero announced proudly, "It's my turn to buy the next bottle." The store clerk told him that they had already finished off his entire inventory. The group of divers left for the next village to find more booze, growing larger as more friends were invited to come along.

Alcero explained, "I have a lot of friends who invite me." Acknowledging that, he added, "After I'm invited, it's a privilege to buy another bottle for the group." He confided in me, "The problem is, I'm invited everywhere I go."

Daugoberto, a Responsible Diver

Daugoberto was Kuka Denecela's grandson, a Kuri buzo in his late twenties. He had years of experience diving and no longer wasted all of his cash vagando. He spent a few hundred to a thousand lempiras partying when he returned to shore but then gave most of his earnings to his wife, children, mother, sisters, or grandmother, the money being split about equally between his wife and members of his mother's matrilocal group. Daugoberto also had outside girlfriends and a semi-permanent concubine. He claimed not to routinely give money to these women. Instead, he waited for a big trip when he earned 10,000–12,000 lempiras (U.S. $725–$870) and then gave one of them enough money (7,000 lempiras, or U.S. $507) to build a house. Daugo said he liked to wait to give big presents because time would tell if a woman was trustworthy. Divers often feared that women feigned affection and thus took advantage of them for their money.

Experienced and mature buzos like Daugo used their big earnings to invest in items like cayucos, motors, houses, or cows. Once Daugo even used the money from a successful diving trip to buy a large quantity of cocaine. He paid 8,000 lempiras (U.S. $580) and then sold it to someone in Barra Patuca for double the price. Daugo, however, claimed that he never sold cocaine again—not because he considered this work morally wrong but because he believed breaking the law was a dangerous way to earn a living. Daugo used his winnings to purchase goods that made a difference in his family's life. Given this, he was considered a "real man" and a responsible diver.

I remember the day that Daugoberto was leaving for sea. He stood on his Aunt Delfina's patio and said his goodbyes to Delfina, Tomasa, Ilabia, and me. While giving each of us the customary Miskitu kiss, which consisted of touching cheeks accompanied by a swift sniff of the other's cheek, he asked us to pray for his safe return. He then handed each of the other women a bunched-up wad of money, an amount I could not decipher from where I was standing. He then turned toward me and did something that stopped me in my tracks. He put a 100-lempira note (about U.S. $7) in my hand and said, "This is for your frescos (sodas)," which he knew that I bought daily from stores.

Embarrassed that a relatively poor person, compared to myself, was giving me their hard-earned money, I became visibly uncomfortable and tried to give it back. Before I could lift my arm, Delfina pinched my elbow while whispering in my ear, "Keep it, you'll insult him if you give it back."

FEELING USED AND ABUSED

Divers with cash in their pockets commonly fear that women want them only for their money. A general distrust of women prevails among men. Many of the divers' insecurities are well founded, as many women claim not to want a penniless man hanging around the house. The buzo song presented below describes how a diver falls in love with a woman named Minerva and spends all of his money partying with her and giving her gifts. The song ends with

Minerva abandoning the diver after he spends all of his money.[5] Minerva then selects another man with funds to stay the night. The first diver, the one singing the song, ends up penniless, heartbroken, and sporting a hangover. Men admitted to their distrust of women, claiming that the Kuri women were promiscuous and routinely slept with other men for the money.

Minerva mairin	**Minerva (woman)**
Kabu wina balri	I came from the sea
auyara ulri	I rode [my canoe] to the beach
wapi wapi wari	I went walking along
tuman latkara dingwari	and entered the patio of Tuman disco
mair nani alilal auya kan	there were lots of women
tila wina kumi laik takri	but out of all of them, I liked only one
ai nina ai win	she told me her name
Minerva makikan	her name was Minerva
mairin luhpia pain kan	she was a fine little woman
Minerva mairin	Minerva (woman)
mairin painkira	the beautiful woman
Minerva mairin	Minerva (woman)
butkuki alpia mairka	my little pigeon
absungki mairin	my little flower
upla nani tilara	out of all the people
man baman kaikri	I only saw you
wapra luhpia naiskira	your little walk is so sweet
bila baikra painkira	your voice is so fine
Minerva mairin	Minerva (woman)
mairin painkira	the beautiful Minerva
yua wala titan kan	the next day at sunrise
tuman na latkara	outside of Tuman disco
wapanka muhntara	beneath the corridor
ai karwi tauwi	I spun around
ventana plikri	and peered through the window
yakan pali praui kan	only to find
Minerva na mairka	that Minerva (woman)
waikna wala bri wan	had picked up another guy

Minerva mairka	Minerva (woman)
saura ai munram na	you did me wrong
waikna wala brisa	you are with another man
saura ai munram	you did me wrong
waitlara balri	I came back to my house
beso kum sin apu	I did not have even a kiss
shilin kum sin apu	I did not have even a cent
saura ai munram na	you did me wrong
Minerva mairin	Minerva (woman)

Men most dramatically fear that their spouses would not mourn their death if they were killed at sea. Several divers explained that their wife would be happy if they died because lobster-boat captains bequeath a diver's wife a large sum of money as compensation for his death. The amount paid depends on the skill of the lobster diver, with deductions made for the price of the funeral. In 2010 a diver's family was paid some 87,000 lempiras (after subtracting about 30,000 lempiras for his funeral) (unpublished document, in the author's possession).

In the following song a Miskitu diver-singer tells of his own demise due to Mermaid sickness. I transcribed these verses from a CD I purchased in 2010. The singer, Larry Morales, lives in the town of Cocobila, near Kuri, and like other singers in Moskitia he has begun to sell his recordings.[6] The lyrics describe what happens when a diver dies at sea and how only the diver's mother is there to care for his body and prepare it for burial. The song more broadly warns other divers that their girlfriends and wives will abandon them after their legs become paralyzed and that only their mother will stay with them.

Kabura wari	**I went out to sea**
Kabura wari	I went out to sea
auya tanira tauri	I turned toward the beach
kabu ripka kriwikan	the waves were breaking
muhnta tanira tauri	I turned to the south
mamiki mairin inikan	my mother was crying
surungki twilki	I carried my backpack
dwarka unra balki	to the edge of the canoe
sari pali taki ini maka balan	I got so sad, I cried to come back again

"Aligueta" ripka ai briwan	the Aligueta wave brought me out to sea
Pedro banko ai briwan	it brought me to the Pedro bank
Ki Gorda bankora ai briwan	it brought me to Key Gorda
Iniorda bankora ai briwan	it brought me to the Iniorda bank
Roselin bankora ai briwan	it brought me to the Roselin bank
Tres Nueve bankora ai briwan	it brought me to the Tres Nueve bank
kabura wari painika wiri	I told my partner I was going to sea
dwarka alawas tankam mangki	to lower the canoe in the water
barrikam mangki	and put the tanks in
mayari wapi	and I went underwater
andat paun kum ikaia	to kill a hundred pounds [of lobster]
pas tingni wari	at the first creek
andat paun kum dingki	I got a hundred pounds at the first creek
sikan tingni dingwari	on the second entrance in the water
sari pali takan	something awful happened
wini ba kaikri taim	when I looked at my body
pain lika ai daukras	it really wasn't good
dia ai daukisa	what's going on?
ai maskara bilara tala man takisa	the mask filled with blood
mahka bot ai briwas	take me to the boat
wini saura ai daukisa	my body is injured
aihka ai daukisa	I'm hurting bad
radiuku lakikan pruan briaula	the radio announced
hielo briaulaki	a dead diver was arriving and to bring ice
dia duri dakban hielo briaula	get any cayuco to put ice in [for the body]
Brus lakun lalmara	just north of Brus Lagoon
butka ba dim balana	another boat was arriving
mangki bribal ulan	to bring my body back
yaptiki inikan	my mother was crying
ai yapti nit dukiara	for my mother's needs
kabura wari	I went out to sea

painika nani turi kumi mai wisni	my friend, I'll tell you a story
mairin sat sat dukiamra	for all kinds of women
kabura wari	I went out to sea
mampta pruan taim	but when your legs are paralyzed
mair nani aihka	the women don't respond well
siam ba man plaplaisa	they get scared and run away from you
krikri ai plikuma	when they have to put you on the bed
bara man yapti lika lamara balki	only your mother stays near you
takisa kan klin munisa	only she bathes you
unan laya dikisa	she wipes away your drool
wan yapti baman	only our mothers
wan ilpka takisa	give us help
kabura wari	I went out to sea

In a recent song by Honduran Miskitu singer Romel Cruz, he sings of a boat owned by Captain Luís, which burned at sea, killing six divers. The song explains the terror the divers experienced while trying to escape from the boat before it exploded, how devastated the mothers of the dead divers were, and how the men's wives and girlfriends did not morn their death. Cruz mentions that the divers' spouses did not even wear black clothing after their death, which is considered appropriate behavior for a spouse. The lyrics from Captain Luís reveal the loneliness that divers feel in their conjugal relationships and underscore the close bonds a man has with his mother.

Kiaptan Luís	Captain Luís
Kiaptan Luís aman taim	When Captain Luís caught afire
sibin aklak awar kan	it was seven o'clock
buzo nani ba sait sait yakawikan	the divers side by side dove off [the boat]
kayuk nani ba sait sait yakawikan	the canoemen side by side dove off
anira swak takaia?	where could they go to save themselves?
tanka briras apu kan	no one knew the answer

yapti nani ba	the mothers
ba torka walan taim	when they heard the story
auya minara takiwi	walked to the beach barefoot
ai lamara kwasi	they crawled on their chests
ai lulara kwasi	they crawled on their knees
auya karbi kan	they dug holes in the sand
upla wala nani ba	the other people
maisin iki watauki kan	gathered to console them
mairin nani ba	the women spouses
piksa winka waras kan	did not go to the bodies
kwala siksa daiki	they took off their black clothes
krikrika muhntara lulkan	and threw them beneath the bed
ai mina pata lulki swin	they kicked them and left them there
yaptik mairin baman	only the mothers
ai maisara wilkisa	morn and need consoling
yaptik mairin baman	only the mothers

In the song below, "Ibilita mairin" (Ibilita woman), the man singing believes that his wife, Ibilita, wants to bury him even before his velorio (wake) has ended. The man pleads with her to wait at least the traditional twenty-four hours to bury him, or at least until his friends arrive. The song illustrates men's deepest fears, that Kuri women are not saddened after their husbands die and, at times, will bring harm and death to their men.[7]

Ibilita Mairin	**Ibilita woman**
tisku naihka walma	In a while you'll hear
wahma pruan walma	the death of a young man
tisku naihka walma	in a while you'll hear
silak binka walma	the sound of the hammer [building a coffin]
Ibilita mairinka	Ibilita (woman)
ai kaiki kapram	you'll be looking at me
nara kama ki?	will you be over here?
bara kama ki?	will you be over there?
Ibilita Mairin	Ibilita (woman)
ai kaiki kapram	you were looking at me

mair nani kunin ini kataihka	when the women cry, they're lying
ai bikpara	don't bury me
mair nani kunin ini kataihka	the women's tears are lies
ai bikpara	don't bury me
ai bikpara	don't bury me
Ibilita mairin	Ibilita (woman)
Kuri wina mairin	the woman from Kuri
ai bikuma ki?	are you really going to bury me?
24 alkras kan ai bikuma na	before twenty-four hours have passed
ai bikuma ki?	are you going to bury me?
24 alkras kan	when not even a day has passed
kakaira mairin balras kan	my female friends have not yet arrived
ai bikuma na	you are going to bury me
Ibilita mairinka	Ibilita (woman)
Kuri wina mairin	the woman from Kuri
prias bilka ini ba	when the church bell rings
ai bikuma ki?	are you going to bury me?
ya bikuma ki?	who are you going to bury?
Ibilita mairinka	Ibilita (woman)
Kuri wina mairin	the woman from Kuri

A buzo-singer named Silin Tailor from the village of Tasbapauni, near Kuri, performed a song that I recorded in 2001. In "Sia ai bripari" (Don't be scared of me), the divers explains that his wife or girlfriend will not come close to his body after death. The song states that generally the women's tears are lies and that they commonly rush their husband's wake in order to bury him sooner.

Sia ai bripari	Don't be scared of me
Sia ai bripari	Don't be scared of me
ai sia brismaki	are you scared of me?
dia muni dahlin	why oh why darling
sia ai brismaki	are you scared of me?
kauhla takri bara	when I [my body] turned cold
sia ai brismaki	were you scared of me?
sia ai bripari	don't be scared of me

raiti bilara lapta sa	it's hot in the cemetery
raiti bilara tihmia sa	it's nighttime in the cemetery
sia ai bripari	don't be scared of me
kaula takri bara	when I turned cold
si brin mai daukan	you were scared
yuli kahbram	accompanying
yang winki na	my body here
lalah tara waiknika	the money man
si brin ai daukisa	you're scared of
sia bripari	don't be scared
mahka auna na	I'm going away now, dying
laimara balras	you don't come near me
sia bripari	don't be afraid
24 alkras kaka	if twenty-four hours have not passed
ai bikpara	don't bury me
mair nani kunin ini kaka	if the women are crying, they are lying
ai bikpara	don't bury me yet

Songs from the Old Days

Two older songs that I recorded tell stories of Río Plátano men working in the cash-based subsistence and canoe-making economies. In the first song a man tells his wife that he will make money from agricultural work to provide her with a home, food, money, and store-bought goods. It demonstrates that men traditionally have been expected to provide resources to women.

Dahlin painkira	**Beautiful darling**
Dahlin painkira	Beautiful darling
na klakla naihka man yaurkam nasla	this arm will be your yucca field
na klakla naihka man platkam nasla	this arm will be your plantain field
na klakna naihka man siksikam nasla	this arm will be your banana field

dahlin painkira	beautiful darling
na klakla naihka man binskam nasla	this arm will be your bean field
na klakla naihka man yauhrakam nasla	this arm will be your yucca field
na klaika naihka man duskam nasla	this arm will be your orchard field
dahlin painkira	beautiful darling
na klakla naihka man wampla si	this arm will be your house
na klakla naihka man lalahkam si	this arm will be your money
na klakla naihka man kwalkam si	this arm will be your clothes
dahlin painkira	beautiful darling
dahlin painkira	beautiful darling

The following song, "Arelita mairin," describes a Miskitu man working in the mahogany canoe-carving business. It tells of a man leaving for the forest who plans to extract mahogany trees and carve them into cayucos. It also recounts his plan to sell the canoes in a local market. "Arelita mairin" demonstrates that men make money in the canoe-building industry, which they in turn proffer to women.[8]

Arelita mairin	**Arelita woman**
Klaura na auni	I am going upriver
Arelita mairin	Arelita (woman)
unta tara na dimauni	I am entering the forest
dori paskaya dimauni	I am going to build cayucos
Arelita mairin	Arelita (woman)
duri nani na sakri	I made some cayucos
wal, yumpa sakri	I finished two or three
Arelita mairin	Arelita (woman)
bili kaiki was	wait for me
Arelita mairin	Arelita (woman)
yua nani lui kan	days have passed
wik nani lui kan	weeks have passed
kati nani luan kan	months have passed
kli tauwi auni	I'm on the way back

Arelita mairinka	Arelita (woman)
bili kaiki was	wait for me
na dwarka naihka	this cayuco will later
man lalkam si	be your money
na dwarka naihka	this cayuco
man sentkam si	is your future cash
Arelita mairin	Arelita (woman)
man lalkam si	it is your money

Another song from the old days, "Yang nani sika yang nani" (We are who we are), was more recently recorded by Honduran Miskitu singer Romel Cruz but tells of Miskitu men's perception of themselves as wage earners and proprietors of several subsistence and cash-based resources. In the first verse the song relates the pride that men feel in being the "owners" of local resources. In the second the singer reaffirms the value of Miskitu men's work by mentioning that companies from the United States pay them for extracting resources.

Yang Nani Sika Yang Nani	**We are who we are**
Yang nani sika yang nani	We are who we are
yang nani sika kangst dawanka	we are the conch owners
yang nani sika labsta dawanka	we are the lobster owners
yang nani sika wahsi dawakna	we are the shrimp owners
yang nani sika dusa nani dawanka	we are the tree owners
yang nani sika inska nani dawanka	we are the fish owners
yang nani sika kuswika nani dawanka	we are the turtle owners
yang nani sika sula nani dawanka	we are the deer owners
yang nani sika kakamuk nani dawanka	we are the iguana owners
ritska ailal bara sa	there are many riches here
ritska ailal bara sa	there are many riches here
Tech nani bal dimi	the U.S. people arrive
naisin nani sat sat balaia	many countries arrive
wan ikbaia dukiara	for us to extract these resources

The three songs that I collected from the "old days," "Arelita mairin," "Dahlin painkira," and "Yang nani sika yang nani," suggest that indigenous gender ideologies have not changed significantly. Together, they demonstrate that

Miskitu men's role as a resource provider predates the lobster economy. Three of the last booming economies in Moskitia—logwood trees, green-sea turtles, and lobsters—are mentioned in the song. Therefore, the idea of men acting as resource provider and household breadwinner has remained more or less constant in Miskitu society.

Interactions with outside economies and market capitalism have shaped the Plátano Miskitu people's gendered identities and their notions of sexuality and power. In the case of the Miskitu people, these effects started long ago. For the past two hundred years, men have worked in foreign economies and have served as the main breadwinner in the household, providing cash and store-bought goods to their family. Songs from before the lobster diving industry began demonstrate that Miskitu manhood revolved around the notion of man as resource provider. Therefore, the social construction of Miskitu manhood has not changed dramatically since the lobster economy began. What is new is the way Miskitu manhood has become more intensely linked to being a lobster diver: being a real man means participating in the dangerous but lucrative lobster-diving occupation. Miskitu boys begin testing their manhood by working as a cayuquero and then later become a buzo. Back on dry land, boys continue transitioning to men by participating in conspicuous consumption and the "giving it all away" prestige economy. The lobster divers feel intensely inadequate when they are lalah apu (flat broke), and they have developed a deep distrust for women, who they believe try to take advantage of them for their wages. My research also reveals that every diver's life has a price tag. If a diver dies at sea, the boat owners pay a sum to the man's family based on his skill level as a diver. This furthers my discussion of the way that men's gender identities have been commodified within the lobster economy. An almost complete mercantilization of masculine bodies has transpired in coastal Miskitu society.

PART III

Supernatural Women

CHAPTER SIX

For the Love of Money

Sex and Magic

MISKITU WOMANHOOD TRADITIONALLY WAS MEASURED BY A woman's ability to be a good mother and to keep her family healthy. With the rise of the lobster economy, being a woman has come to do with one's ability to garner cash resources from men. A real woman must gain access to a diver's money in order to be a good mother and keep her household economically afloat. Many women procure money from the male divers through the practice of mairin mana (literally, women's pay or salary), an expression that refers to the exchange of money for sexual relations. Miskitu women also regularly utilize a variety of sexual magic potions called praidi saihka (plant-based, supernatural remedies), which manipulate men's emotions and behaviors.[1] Once used for love, magic potions are now used for more purely economic reasons. This chapter demonstrates that women's relationships with men have been commercialized, further developing my thesis that commodified gender and sexual identities have taken hold within the lobster economy.

Mairin mana, a cash gift of money, is a special type of present that women receive from lobster divers. Miskitu divers frequently give their lovers between ten and twenty-five U.S. dollars after engaging in sexual relations. A strong belief predominates that this money is a prisant (present). A real man does not meddle with the day-to-day running of a woman's household. The phrase *tuktan mana* (children's payment), a less commonly used expression for mairin mana, underlines the fact that the gift of money will go toward feeding the woman's children. The following is an example of a mairin mana exchange.

A buzo approaches a woman's house in the night (without igniting his flashlight) and lightly knocks on the door.

"Man ya?" (Who is it?), a woman inquires.

"Yang" (It's me), the diver responds.

The diver purposefully does not speak his name aloud in case another man is inside the house. When a woman is already with another man, she says, "Go away, I'm sleeping." If alone, she may let the diver in for the night. Women turn away drunken divers or make them slip money under the door before being allowed to enter. More commonly, divers leave their gifts of cash before departing. If the diver respects the woman's reputation, he will covertly exit before dawn so that the neighbors will not see him.[2]

Mairin mana seems to be a part of the divers' ritualized behavior of giving (see chapter 5), in which men provide resources and cash to the women they love or desire. A woman views the gift of money as a symbol of love and affection, proof that the man cares about her. A woman in Kuri confessed to me, "A man giving cash is a man giving his heart." The situation that I observed in Moskitia seems parallel to Janet Siskind's (1973) study in the Peruvian Amazon, where Cashinahua women and men in the same community traded sex for meat. Siskind reports that the men were commonly the boyfriends, secret lovers, and husbands of the Cashinahua women. Miskitu women seem to have merely replaced meat (and other subsistence items) with the newer resource of cash in an economy of desire. Grandmothers may arrange for these relationships to develop between their grown daughters and their suitors, often suggesting the amount of an adequate donation. In this way, senior women maintain control of the cash-based resources in the matrigroup.

Most of the literature on sex work focuses on the globalized sex-tourism industry, where sexual exchange encounters take place between brown bodies from the global South and white voyager-consumers from the global North

(Brennan 2004; Kempadoo 2003). The Plátano Miskitu case of commodified affection differs significantly from this mainstream focus on "sex work" in the Caribbean. My work documents an economy of desire in which the exchange of money and sexual relations transpires within an indigenous society. J. Peter Figueroa (2008) and Barry Chevannes (2001) similarly suggest that poor women in Jamaica trade sex for social support. Chevannes (2001:198) quotes a popular Jamaican saying: "Men need sex, which women have: women need money, which men must find to satisfy their demand." Wekker (2006) shows that Surinam women also entered into romantic relationships with older men and women for financial reasons. Kamala Kempadoo (2009) refers to this practice as transactional sex, which she believes is linked to poverty and increased consumerism. Kempadoo (2009:4) defines transactional sex as:

> relationships that involve a deliberate exchange of sex for some form of "betterment"—material goods, clothes, accommodation, social status, and so forth—but are not viewed by the people involved as prostitution, and are not typically based on notions of romance or love. These usually involve young women with older men, but include teenage boys with older women.
>
> The extent and range of sexual-economic relations in the region are not easily determined, for they encompass a wide variety of activities and exchanges and, due to their illegal and stigmatized character, are not widely acknowledged. . . . In such studies, a notion of sexual intercourse as "work" appears regularly, leading to conceptualizations of the exploitation, trade, or sale of sexual labour. It is also here that female (hetero) sexual agency appears, most commonly coupled to poor women's strategies to "make do."

The practice of transactional sex has provoked scholars of Latin America and the Caribbean to reconsider their definition of "sex work." Researchers now differentiate between prostitution and the exchange of sex for social and economic support. This allows us to view Miskitu women's transactional relationships with Miskitu lobster divers as distinct from prostitution. Miskitu people themselves do not view mairin mana encounters as prostitution. Those classed as prostitutes (urkira) live in the larger towns and make a living exclusively (or nearly so) by receiving cash for sex. Prostitutes also take birth control, have a set price for sexual relations, require prepayment, and do not have emotional ties with their clients. Conversely, Kuri women who accept mairin mana participate in these behaviors only a few times a month for a portion of their income, do not use birth control, and do not attach a set price to sex. Locals claim that mairin mana is further distinguished from professional prostitution because Miskitu men give money to women after, not before, the sexual encounter, in the spirit of a donation to the woman's household. Even diverging from Kempadoo's definition of transactional sex, many of the relationships are based in romance; Miskitu women are frequently in love with their late-night visitors. Moreover, a woman who becomes pregnant from a mairin mana encounter will give the child the last name of the man, who becomes recognized publicly as the father. Many of the men with whom Miskitu women choose to sleep are already the father of their children; and women often hope to have more children with the man.

The Kuka and the Lobster Diver

Daugoberto, a Miskitu lobster diver in his late twenties, stood on the beachfront patio of his Aunt Delfina's cookhouse. Delfina, the eldest daughter of Kuka Denecela, was quickly usurping Kuka's power, owing to the fact that she married Siksto George, the first native Miskitu elementary schoolteacher in Honduras. Avoiding eye contact with his aunts and grandmother, Daugo gazed out to the Caribbean Sea. He combed his fingers through his rusty, sun-bleached hair before speaking. Finally, he turned toward the group to tell them what they were waiting to hear:

> *Men have to make their own decisions. That's what makes them men. If a man wants to leave one day, he just packs his backpack and goes when and where he pleases. . . . No one owns me; I'm my own boss. I'm a lobster diver. No woman is going to tell me what to do. I have women and children all over Moskitia . . . in Nicaragua, Jamaica, and the Bay Islands, too. When I want to see them, I just pick up and go and no wife of mine is going to say anything—as long as she has a roof over her head and food on the table for the children, what can she say? If Delbia complains, I'll stay away longer [and not give her any money]. That will make her think [learn a lesson].*

The several women present did not respond, not even Kuka Denecela, who everyone knew disapproved of Daugo's recent abandonment of his wife. Kuka

Denecela was not only Daugo's grandmother (Daugo's father's mother), but she was also his wife, Delbia's, anti, or aunt (her mother's sister's cousin). Kuka did not want her niece and great-grandchildren living in a female-headed household without a cash provider. She fully realized that men alone had access to steady wages as lobster divers.

A few days later Kuka sat on a bench in her cookhouse, peeling yucca with an oversized butcher knife. Next to her crouched her sister, Mama Tara (literally, Big Mother), a short, rotund woman with dark skin and smiling eyes. Mama Tara, the conjoining matrigroup's grandmother, was one of only seven true shamans, or suhkia, in the entire coastal region.

Attempting to have a private conversation with Mama Tara, Kuka Denecela fired off commands to keep the older and wiser children out of earshot: "Doralicet, haul some water. . . . Rustelia, hang the clothes outside. . . . Mario, leña (pine wood)." Kuka exchanged her butcher knife for a wooden pipe and lighted the tobacco leaf with a sliver of burning pine wood. Exhaling a long stream of smoke, she reflected on Daugoberto and Delbia's impending separation: "Listen. If Daugo doesn't go back to his wife and children by his own will, I'll make him go back with one of my magic potions. He won't have a choice then. He'll never want to leave Delbia's house or her food again. He won't be able to stand it for one minute without the sight of her face. Daugo's going to follow her to the bathroom when she goes to defecate. We'll see how much of his own boss he is."

Taken together, the above statements by Daugo and Kuka reflect social discord in Miskitu gender and power relations. Daugo's first comments (said in public to his family) revealed the power that men have as Miskitu society's main wage earners. Kuka's statements (said in private to her sister, a shaman) illustrated the power that Miskitu women maintain in matrilocal groups and the way that women use magic potions (sihka) and the broader discourse surrounding magic to contest the region's male-dominant lobster economy.

Considering the gender and power contradictions that women and men experience in their daily lives, this story about Kuka and Daugoberto is instructive. In the end Kuka did use sexual magic to coerce Daugo into returning to his wife and children. Here we see the ideological discourse that allows Miskitu society to maintain its equilibrium. Sexual magic, and the discourse surrounding it, is the deep structure that keeps gender and power contradictions from tearing apart Miskitu society, especially as it becomes increasingly more involved in the cash economy.

After years of living closely with women in Kuka Denecela's matrigroup, I became aware of the pervasive use of sexual magic, or praidi saihka, by mothers and grandmothers. Sexual magic is a way that women retain control of cash resources for the matrigroup. Senior women, who control the recipes for the potions, manipulate young men's emotions to influence marriage, divorce, and ultimately the standard of living of their daughters' households. Miskitu grandmothers are both respected and feared by others in society for possessing the knowledge associated with sexual magic. The kukas pass down highly guarded secrets of praidi saihka to their daughters and granddaughters in the private domain of the matrigroup. Given that the incantations and recipes vary widely, different matrigroups become associated with certain types of sexual magic. Knowledge of specific sexual magic recipes and incantations has become a central component of Miskitu cultural identity and female power in coastal villages (Cunningham 2003; L. Herlihy 2005, 2006; see also Few 2002; Lewis 2003).

"Praidi saihka" literally means "Friday's medicine" in the Miskitu language. "Praidi" (Friday) is a word clearly borrowed from the English language. "Saihka" is a form of the noun "sihka" (medicine or healing remedy), marked for possession.[3] Kuri locals also call the magic potions *winsdi saihka* (Wednesday's medicine) because they contend that the plant spirits listen to requests from humans on both Fridays and Wednesdays, which are the two best and holiest days for making sexual magic.[4] Since men are the most common recipients of the bewitching potions, some women casually refer to the supernatural potions as *waikna saihka* (man medicine). Kuri men also have access to magic potions, but they most commonly used potions defensively, to block or cut the effect of women's sexual magic potions or to protect them from the Mermaid. Men also use potions to help them find lobsters and to increase their strength while fighting other men (Pérez Chiriboga 2002). Moreover, men who have emigrated to the coast from outside of the region are separated from the women healers in their natal matrigroup, which decreases their access to magic potions.

Women mainly use the potions to control men's emotions and behaviors—the potions most typically bewitch men into falling in love with a woman, beguile them into giving cash and other gifts, and bewilder them by erasing their memories of former wives and children. Women often use sexual magic in conjunction with mairin mana encounters in order to ensure that they receive a more generous cash present from a man after sexual relations. Mothers principally employed sexual magic potions to attract the wealthier and more desirable wahmas (young men) for their daughters and to chase off unwanted suitors. Jamieson (2000) reports that in Nicaragua Miskitu women control the sexuality of their adolescent daughters by choosing their daughters' suitors and determining the proper mate. The mothers control the young men, according to Jamieson, through a joking relationship and kid the young men in public about their sexual prowess. My work demonstrates that mothers also use sexual magic as a method of control over young men.

TYPES OF POTIONS

There are three major categories of praidi saihka: *aisi sakaia*, which involves a money payment to a plant, extracting or cutting the plant, and saying an oration; *yabakaia*, which requires an additional element of ritualized blowing; and *yumuh*, the most potent, which demands more complicated ingredients and is more prayer-oriented (Barrett 1992; Dennis 1988; García 1996a; House and Sánchez 1997). Locals prefer the more ethereal yumuh because these sihka cannot be easily diffused with a counteractive potion. All three forms of sexual magic require incantations to imbue the potions with supernatural powers.

At midday (10:00 a.m.) on Wednesdays or Fridays, women furtively walk to the patio or lagoon and pay a plant a sum of money so that the plant spirit will listen to them. They first place money (one to five U.S. dollars) under a root or stalk of the plant as an offering. They then pray to the plant spirit, extract the plant part needed, and use the plant to make a concoction. To render the potion into a supernatural remedy, women recite an incantation and sometimes blow air (*puhbaia*) in a quick and patterned way. They repeat these actions on the following two Wednesdays or Fridays at midday for two types of potions (aisi sakaia and yabakaia), but for another type (yumuh) the incantation is recited three days in a row (Wednesday, Thursday, and Friday).

Abbreviated versions of the incantations for the most common potions are presented below, along with an explanation of the situations in which women employ each potion. All of these potions are used by women to control men and achieve their economic goals.

Yamni kaikan (love potion): Women and men most frequently use yamni kaikan in their attempt to manipulate people (men, women, elders, and children) and even dogs into loving them. Currently, women living in coastal villages typically utilize this broad-spectrum love potion to charm multiple lobster divers into giving them cash or presents, like cokes, snacks, or clothes.

Yamni kaikan	Love potion
Yamni kaikan man	Love potion
yamni kaikan man	love potion you
waikna kang ai kaikbia	at the minute a man sees me
tuktan kang ai kaikbia	at the moment a child sees me
mairin kang ai kaikbia	at the moment a women sees me
yul kang ai kaikisa	at the moment a dog sees me
daiwan kang ai kaikbia	at the moment an animal sees me
upla ulsut ul tawan yamni kaikan	everybody, the whole town, love
plis tnata wahl-wahl yamni kaikan	at the four corners of the place, love
daiwan kang ai kaikbia	at the moment an animal will see me,
drin prubia	it will faint
umpira kaikan yumika	love potion's yumuh
naiwra mai yabakisna	today I pray to you

Ai lihkan (love potion): Another kind of love potion, ai lihkan is similar to yamni kaikan. However, an ai lihkan spell is focused on one special person. Many Kuri women were known for having used ai lihkan to seduce a lobster diver and garner his resources.

Stand-bai (love potion): Stand-bai (standby) has power to coerce a man into being overly attentive to a woman's every need. Kuri women warned me that this medicine must be used with caution because a man who is spellbound becomes so attached that he does not let the woman out of his sight, even following her to the bathroom. Women consider this undesirable because they value having free time away from their husbands to *kirbaia* (to go out and socialize) with female friends and relatives.

Amia tikaia (memory eraser): Amia tikaia is a potion that erases one's memories of former relationships. Women often combine amia tikaia with a hate potion (misbara) to steal a man away from his wife and children. While the hate potion ensures that a man will leave his wife and children, the amia tikaia wipes out his memory of them. As described in chapter 3, many men born and raised in other regions come to the coast to work as lobster divers and marry locally. Their Miskitu wives in Kuri may give them amia tikaia so that they forget their former families and, more important, do not send money to them. "He won't even remember his own mother," Kuka Livian declared. For a wife living on the coast, amia tikaia secures her man's constant presence in her household, so that his labor and resources will be available for the matrilocal group.

Kupia ikaia (anti-jealousy potion): Meaning literally "to kill the heart," kupia ikaia is a potion that prevents a man from being jealous or too protective of his wife. The potion also coerces men into doing household chores and handling childcare while their spouse has trysts with, and accept money from, other men. Kupia ikaia provides a woman with the opportunity to have it all—a husband, a boyfriend, and access to both of their resources.

Utla almuk	**Old house**
Utla sukra man	You old house
Natalio ba Nora ahbras kabia	Natalio will not get mad at Nora
aisaia wihka ahbras kabia	when they talkin' the future, he won't get mad
utla sukra man	you old house
man sika saut krauhi luan	you medicine, when the south wind blew
ahbras bui katma ba baku	you took away the anger
diwas krauhi luan	the wind blew past, leaving the land for the sea,
ahbras katma ba	you [Natalio] won't be mad
kwal tara bal maki alki luan	a big squall comes, grabs you, and then releases you
ahbras bui katma ba baku	like you won't get mad
prari tara ba mai alki knamptara	a big hurricane grabs you to the end
slukbi mai ikan	destroying and almost killing you
muntamra suklung dimikan	beneath you a frog entered without getting angry
ahbras Norara ahbras kabia	you will not get angry at Nora
naiwra mai alkisa	today this spell takes hold

Kaiura ikaia (anti-virility potion): Kaiura ikaia means "to kill the yucca (yam, *Dioscorea*)," a metaphor for the penis. This potion takes away a man's virility, and women use kaiura ikaia to prevent their spouse from committing an infidelity. A man who has been hexed is still able to have relations with his wife, but this potion prevents him from having sexual relations with and giving his money away to another woman. Even when the man feels physically attracted to a woman, he will be unable to attain an erection. Knowledge of how to concoct both the kupia ikaia and the kaiura ikaia potions is highly guarded, and women who know these potions are considered especially threatening and treacherous.

Almuk mahabra	Old eggs testicles
Almuk mahabra	Old eggs testicles
almuk nani ailal mahabra man	old person, lots of years testicles you
man Natalio mairinra wabia	when Natalio takes his out for a woman
ai pismaut alabia taim dama	it will go down like a grandfather
"cien años" baku kabia	one hundred years old
diera daukbia apia	he will be able to do nothing
sukra baku kabia	it will be too mature and worn
almuk yumuhka man	you old person potion you
dama pismaut yumuhka man	grandfather shrinking out potion you

Wauwisa (beckoning potion): Wauwisa (whirling through the air) is a potion that beckons one from afar. If the wind is blowing in the right direction, the intended man will be touched on the cheek by the wauwisa, which then tantalizes him into coming directly to the woman who sent it. Women are said to use wauwisa when a man is a migrant wage-laborer, to entice him into returning home before he spend his pay on or falls in love with another woman. Some elderly women claim that they utilized this potion in the past, when Miskitu men worked in Belize for lumber and fruit companies.

Wauwisa	Whirling through the air
Wauwisa man	Whirling through the air you
Nora ba yabi si kupia tak krauhka	Nora sending this will cause a sudden memory
Natalio kat ai kupia lukbia	all the way to Natalio, he will remember me
yapi si kupia dan kropa boka	when he falls asleep it will enter his heart
Natalio kat ai kupia lukbia	to Natalio he will remember me
wauwisa man puram luras	whirling through the air you, you will not fail

kupia ba karbi lak man	you will twist his heart around
yapisi kupia kraubi wina	after he sleeps, he will remember
aimiara lukbiara kaka	when he thinks of his wife
plapli wi bara baku	he will run to her
tingni kaka yui lubia ba	if by stream, he will cross swimming
aras kaka yui lubia ba	if by horse, he will come on top of it
wauwisa man nairwa bakisa	whirling through the air, you, today
	I pray to you
naha tihmia natama bakrik man	tonight, in the middle of the night
wi witin ra prukaia maia bak isna	go and strike Nora's husband
maia bak isna	send this to the husband

Misbara (hate potion): This potion deludes a man or woman into abandoning his or her home. When a woman wants to live with a married man, she uses misbara to make him leave his wife. Many times misbara is stated as the reason for a failed marriage and constitutes a truly no-fault divorce. Locals contend that neither spouse can be blamed for a failed marriage when a third party puts a misbara on the house. The incantation accompanying the potion explains how the potion causes the man to despise his home and gives it an odor to the point that he has to leave.

Misbarka	**Hate potion**
Plis misbarka yumuka man	Place hate potion you
upla pruan misbarka man	dead people hate potion you
kang misbarka man	touch hate potion you
Natalio Kuri pliska na kana krabi	to Natalio, this place Kuri stinks
maka sia plapisma ba baku	and makes him run with fear
upla pruan lapta yumpa	like a dead person on their third day
karas pruan, kia saura brih bisbaya	alligator dead, a bad smell is brought
Kuri pliskara sim plapbia	you will run from Kuri
plis misbarka man	place hate potion you
upla pruan biki si	people die and are buried
maka wih kabia ba baku	after you will go the same way
Nora ba kli watauwi balbia apia	you will not return to Nora ever again
prura misbarka man	death hate potion you
naiwra mai yabakisna	today I pray to you

Women also use misbara potions in combination with other potions. A young woman named Misdina kept Kuri villagers amused by the yearly cycle of sexual magic she employed. Misdina was known for alternately bewitching Benli (the father of her three small children) with yamni kaikan to attract him to her house during the lobster-diving season, when he had money, and then putting a misbara spell on him during the veda, or four-month moratorium on lobster extraction, to send him away from her house when he was broke. More commonly, Kuri women combine yamni kaikan and misbara to steal a man from another woman; a woman would attract the man to her with the love potion while also calling on the hate potion to make the man leave his girlfriend or wife. A few women top this off with amia tikaia to trick the man into forgetting about his former wife and family. This potent combination of three supernatural spells—yamni kaikan, misbara, and amia tikaia—ensures maximum economic gain for the female enchantress.

Some Kuri men did talk to me about their fear of being manipulated by the women's potions and admitted that they purchased counteractive potions and charms as a preventative or prophylaxis.[5] These men claimed that they avoided the female members of the families known for having this expertise. Bullard (1974, in McClaurin 1996:68) points out that in nearby Belize Creole men also fear women's sexuality and use of sexual magic (see also D. Bell 1993). Tension may arise in Miskitu daily life based on men's distrust and suspicion of women's sexual magic. Miskitu men's fear of women's supernatural powers, as seen through their use of counteractive potions, serves to reinforce the idea that women's potions are effective and an important part of their personal and domestic power.

Strategies and Resistance

My research on sexual magic reflects newer, commodified identities for Miskitu women within the lobster economy. The research also presents sexual magic as a strategy that women use successfully to gain access to men's earnings. Kuri men and women were convinced that gifts of money resulted from magic potions that the women used on men. Kuri women told me that lobster divers gave them between U.S. $50 and $200 per month, but they had difficulty linking a dollar amount to the use of a particular potion.[6] Nevertheless, both sexes perceive supernatural potions not just as ritualistic practices that release some frustrations but as a practical way to achieve economic goals (see also Price 1993). Given that Miskitu women do indeed use magic potions to empower themselves economically vis-à-vis men, one may ask whether this is a "true" form of social resistance to patriarchal structures in Miskitu society (J. Scott 1992).

Social scientists and historians view magic or witchcraft as a form of resistance to Spanish colonial society's structures (Lewis 2002). In colonial Mexico, for example, Behar (1987), Noemi Quezada (1984, 1989), and Brenda Rosenbaum (1996) find that Nahua women used sexual magic to contest and subvert the patriarchal gender ideology imposed by the Spanish. Rosenbaum (1996:330) contends that Nahua women practiced "witchcraft" to gain some control and power over their lives, as the church, state, and Spanish ideologies attempted to keep Nahua women submissive. Behar (1987) explains that indigenous women stupefied their husbands with potions and thus beguiled them into ending outside relationships (see also Romanucci-Ross 1993). Behar believes that the double sexual standard that permeated Spanish colonial gender ideology drove women to these ends. Quezada (1984; 1989) mentions that Nahua women employed sexual magic, which she calls *magia amorosa* (love magic), not only to save their marriage but to regain their economic security.[7]

On the Central American Caribbean coast, researchers similarly describe women's use of magic potions to contest patriarchal ideologies (Kerns 1997; McClaurin 1996). Garífuna and Creole men in Belize, like Miskitu lobster divers, exercise their economic power over women by having various girlfriends and wives. Irma McClaurin (1996:121) contends that Garífuna and Creole women in Belize use *Obeah* (magic, in Creole English) to contest their own society's double sexual standard by manipulating their spouses into falling in love with them again. McClaurin also reports that, "a man who seems overly solicitous to a woman is thought to be under the influence of Obeah" (68). Virginia Kerns (1997:91) observes that Belizean women attract or "tie" men to them by putting water used to wash their genitals or their menstrual blood in the men's food. As with the Miskitu use of kupia ikaia and kaiura ikaia, these types of obeah make men impotent with other women. Comparing Nahua and Belizean Creole women's use of sexual magic to that of Miskitu women reveals that Nahua and Belizean women mainly view witchcraft or obeah as justified recourse for men's frequent infidelities. Miskitu women, in contrast, are less concerned with their men's faithfulness and more concerned with their wages.[8] Chevannes (2001) finds that Jamaican women, similar to Miskitu women, value men's money more than their fidelity.

Miskitu women's application of magic potions operates at one level as critique of the capitalist social order and the idea of man as breadwinner. At the same time, women's incantations support the hegemonic gender ideology. Most significantly, women are not using sexual magic to find wage-earning jobs. Instead, women seek to manipulate men who have jobs and money, thus reinforcing male dominance by avoiding the problem of wage earning instead of directly confronting it. Thus women simultaneously contest and reinforce society's male-dominant gender ideology.[9] We can now see the ways in which women manipulate men with magic potions as both resistance and accommodation to the patriarchal gender ideology.

Ethnohistorians Conzemius (1932:145) and Helms (1971:86) report the historic use of "love magic" for more romantic reasons: to attract a lover or win the affection of someone. Today, however, Kuri women primarily use sexual magic to manipulate male lobster divers into giving them gifts of cash. Here we see a new development, women using praidi saihka for their economic survival within the expanding market economy. This represents an important new application of plant-based healing potions (sihka) in Miskitu society. Mairin mana also represents a new strategy that women use to survive as their society becomes more involved with the cash economy. While neither sexual magic nor mairin mana seems to be a true form of resistance, these customs are strong markers of the nature of market-based gender and sexual identities during the long-term boom in the lobster industry.

Subordinate Discourses

Coastal Miskitu women often say in front of others, "Waikna kau pain nu taksa" (Men know best), and also, "Dawan pas, baha wina waikna nani, mairin nani an tuktan nani las" (God first, men second, and women and children last). Both sexes buy into the public discourse of male authority, which is spoken by men and women in stores, discotheques, and village patios, while the subordinate discourse of female autonomy is spoken by women in the private and secretive context of their household.[10] Viewing Miskitu women's sexual magic incantations as a subordinate discourse is helpful for understanding gender politics on the coast. Susan Gal (1991:176–78) believes that marginal, subordinate discourses represent one of many sites of struggle over kinship, gender, and power definitions in societies with patriarchal gender ideologies. Safa (1995) finds that women household heads in the Dominican Republic and Puerto Rico and are primarily responsible for making ends meet. However, the women continue to reinforce the dominant ideology in society that men are the main breadwinners.

The women repeat expressions that claim men are the head of the household, all the while defying this in daily practice. In similar ways, Miskitu women make statements about men being the main resource provider and household head. These cultural expressions are a public display of women's participation in the hegemonic discourse on gender, power, and kinship; they are part of the formal and public transcript that belies women's autonomy in matrilocal groups and their manipulation of men through magic potions.

Power, then, not only is a public phenomenon, as in Western narratives, but also functions in the crafting of everyday social relations (Blackwood 2000:7, 187). Incorporating Michel Foucault's (1980) ideas into gender theory creates a conceptual place from where Miskitu women's power can be theorized. Foucault views power as accessible to those in society not only through the state's controls but also from subordinate, marginalized, or subaltern discourses. Similarly, this research illustrates how power is negotiated and protested in female-headed households in small communities along the remote Honduran Caribbean coast. Here, Miskitu women's power lies beyond the scope of the Honduran state (which recognizes male surnames and men as legitimate heads of households) and westernized religious practices but within the discursive field surrounding matrilocal groups and supernatural potions. This should remind readers of the importance of localized ethnography and how women's strategies in the global economy are situated in their everyday linguistic and healing practices (Tsing 2000).

CHAPTER SEVEN

Fishy Tales

—⇒——————————

The Mermaid

T HE LĪWA MAĪRĪN, OR MERMAĪD, ĪS THE MAĪN MĪSKĪTU WATER spirit (*lasa*), recognized as the owner of all resources in the rivers, lagoons, and sea. Traditionally known for her ability to wreak havoc, mainly on children and animals in the agricultural communities along the Río Plátano, the ocean Mermaid is now infamous for preying on male lobster divers beneath the Caribbean waters. The ocean Mermaid now looms larger than her riverine sister in the hearts and minds of Plátano Biosphere residents; she has become the salient, unmarked liwa (worm-shaped water spirit) in everyday Miskitu discourse. Building on my argument that commodified gender identities have developed in coastal Miskitu society, this chapter focuses on the way the relationship between the ocean Mermaid and Miskitu divers is directly guided by market-based economic principles. Plátano Miskitu men are known for selling their soul to the Mermaid in exchange for the cash-based lobster resource. This exemplifies the commercialized identities that have developed within the lobster economy.

Part goddess and part devil, the Mermaid is Mother Nature's more sadistic and sexy younger sister. She is a supernatural femme fatale who uses her beauty and wealth to enrapture, kidnap, rape, and murder. Mothers warn their children not to bathe or play in the water by saying, "The Mermaid's going to get you." Many stories circulate about men who have gone missing forever. I heard the following abduction story constantly: when the Mermaid likes a man, she seduces him with her beauty and promises of riches and then takes his soul, so that he ceases living among humans and instead lives with her below the water as her lover. Kuka Denecela explained that when a liwa likes a man, she gets to know him in a river, a lagoon, or the sea, begins visiting him at night, and then tries to kidnap him, stealing his soul and taking it away from the human world.[1] Stealing one's soul is a euphemism for killing a person. Kuri residents claim that some men have escaped from the Mermaid's lavish underwater home and have told of her riches under the sea, including large collections of jewels and even speedboats with huge outboard motors.

There are obvious similarities between the liwa mairin and the mermaid of legends espoused by pirates and buccaneers who hid out on the Miskito Coast during the sixteenth through eighteenth centuries (Barrett 1992:347).[2] Yet in Amazonian riverine societies water spirits are believed to seduce and abduct humans to live under the water forever as their spouses (M. Brown 1986:52; Price 1993:xix).[3] The origin of the liwa in Miskitu mythology and folklore dates at least to colonial times, when a synthesis may have occurred between the indigenous and European tradition. What is unique about water spirits in Moskitia is that they have various manifestations, living in different types of waterways and having different races, ages, and genders. Most commonly, liwas affect people of another race and ethnicity, the opposite sex, and the same general age category. Thus their interactions with humans are inherently sexualized and predisposed for both exotic and erotic relationships. While there is also a male water spirit, called *liwa waikna* (the Merman), he does not have the same hold over the Miskitu people's psyche as the Mermaid. This can be explained by the fact that men have more contact with the female water spirit through their water-bound occupations (e.g., fishing, turtling, and lobster hunting) than the more stationary and landlocked women. The Merman's interaction with Kuri women generally was limited to the families who lived close to the saltwater lagoon (Tampa

Tingni) and the freshwater canal, where women of the Kusuapaihka neighborhood wash clothes and bathe.

The riverine Mermaid, the freshwater spirit, resides underwater in the Río Plátano. The riverine Mermaid is described as being of various races, including *liwa mairin siksa* (the black Mermaid), *liwa mairin pauni* (the red Mermaid), and *liwa mairin pihni* (the white Mermaid). These riverine spirits, according to Miskitu and Pech elders, and can turn over canoes, make people sick, or kill them. Fear of the riverine Mermaid often prevents residents from crossing and traversing the Río Plátano. Most commonly, she resides close to a Miskitu family's agricultural camp, where she makes children sick, causes animals to die, and ruins the crops. Many Plátano Miskitu elders told me that the riverine Mermaid first lived near the Pech settlement of Kiajkimina but then moved downriver in the early 1900s to Liwa Raya, a Miskitu agricultural camp.

Verses of the following song, "Liwa mairin" recount how a shaman (suhkia) named Mikitrik twice exorcised the water spirit from the Río Plátano, first from Kiajkimina and then from Liwa Raya, by swimming her out to sea. I collected this song from the musician-diver Wilintin Suárez, who claims to be a descendant of Mikitrik. The song reveals an important part of the Plátano Miskitu people's common mythic history. It also alludes to the historic interactions between the Miskitu and Pech peoples along the middle Río Plátano.[4]

Liwa mairin	**Mermaid**
Liwa mairin, mairin painkira	Mermaid, beautiful woman
tawan yam baku daukram kan	you were doing harm near the town
Kiakimina lamara	near Kiakimina
liwa mairin, liwa mairin	Mermaid, Mermaid
liwa mairin, mairin painkira	Mermaid, beautiful woman
waikna kumi baikan kan	a man was born
Mikitriki makikan	named Mikitrik
liwa mairin, liwa mairin	Mermaid, Mermaid
Mikitriki waikna	Mikitriki was the man
waikna karna makikan	he was called a strong man
natka tara plikan kan	he searched for a powerful way

tawan uplika aikuki	along with the town's people
Liwa mairin, liwa mairin	Mermaid, Mermaid
liwa mairin, mairin painkira	Mermaid, beautiful woman
Ras awalaka bilara	in the Rio Plátano
trabil tara na takan kan	there was a big problem
Pech nani luras kan	the Pech couldn't cross
upla ailal luras kan	many people couldn't cross
liwa mairin, liwa mairin	Mermaid, Mermaid
liwa mairin, mairin painkira	Mermaid, beautiful woman
Mikitriki buan	Mikitriki went upriver
wark karna daukan	he did hard work
liwa mairin, liwa mairin	Mermaid, Mermaid
pliskam wina mai sakan	he kicked you out of your place
mayara baku pali iuram	but you went down below
Liwa Raya pliskara	to Liwa Raya
tasbayam daukram man	you were then harming this place
liwa mairin, liwa mairin	Mermaid, Mermaid
liwa mairin, mairin painkira	Mermaid, beautiful woman
Pech nani buan	The Pech came [to Liwa Raya]
tanka tara plikikan	to try to solve the problem
untaki pliki muni	they searched in the forest
yabal nani na sakikan	they had to find a path
Baltimore pliskaki balki na muni	to arrive to Baltimore
ai yabalka sakan	they chose their path
liwa mairin, liwa mairin	Mermaid, Mermaid
liwa mairin, mairin painkira	Mermaid, beautiful woman
Mikitriki bui kan	Mikitrik came upriver
natka wala pliki kan	to try a different way
Mikitriki buan mai saki	Mikitrik exorcised you
baku mai munan	just like that he did it to you
kabu tanira mai sakan	he took you out to sea
liwa mairin, liwa mairin	Mermaid, Mermaid
liwa mairin, mairin painkira	Mermaid, beautiful woman

When speaking about the ocean or saltwater Mermaid in daily conversation, Miskitu people use the linguistically unmarked category or term "liwa" (water spirit), which refers to the highly eroticized female water spirit with long, blonde hair, white skin, and a body that is half fish and half human.[5] This Mermaid looks like a pretty meriki (Anglo) woman. Kuri residents believe that the ocean Mermaid becomes angry when divers kill too many of her spiny lobsters and, as a result, punishes them with sickness and death.

Lobster divers often suffer from the bends, or decompression sickness, which Miskitu people call liwa mairin sickness. Of all seven hundred lobster divers on the north coast, nearly a hundred (or 15 percent) have been injured or killed on the job, as evidenced by the conspicuously high number of men who walk with limps and crutches or ride in the few available wheelchairs. In larger, more urban Miskitu cities like Bilwi–Puerto Cabezas, Nicaragua, divers have more access to wheelchairs and live more independently; wheelchairs

ESMERALDA (KIAMKSITA)

FIGURE 36.
The Mermaid,
by E. Saession

pass easily on paved streets compared to the beach and savanna foot trails in Honduras. During casual conversations I often asked injured divers (in both Honduras and Nicaragua) what caused their paralysis. Without fail, they would look to the ground with deference and respect and say only one word, "liwa." Many divers claim to have seen or felt the Mermaid underwater, just prior to being stricken with decompression illness—frightened by the sight of her, or even her hair, divers ascend too quickly from the ocean's depths. Divers understand that experiencing a rapid decrease in air pressure is what gives them the bends, but they blame the pernicious water spirit who startles them underwater.

Divers live anxious lives, torn between the coastal women's desire for cash and store-bought goods and the Mermaid, who threatens them with death. They often buy amulets or lobster medicine (*labsta saihka*), which they contend bring them luck while diving. Below is an example of an incantation that brings good luck to divers. However, divers must beware: those who overexploit the lobster resource run a high risk of liwa sickness. Accordingly, the divers often use counteractive potions to protect themselves from the Mermaid. The second text below is part of an incantation to ward off the evil powers of the water spirit.

Labsta saihka tup	**Lobster medicine amulet**
Labsta saihka	Lobster medicine
tup man tangni man	you amulet you flower
ilis man	umbilical cord
tuktan kwalka man	you are my children's clothes
upla biara wina biamra bilara	from a human stomach to your stomach
mangki bri kakma baku	as if placed in your nose
waikna nani anira wabia	the men wherever they go
inska sapa labsta sapa aksbil sapa	it will be fish or lobster or turtle
sut man biamra bilara	you will have all you want to eat
bri kat ma baku	inside your stomach
mihtam bilara aimaks satka ba sut	your hand will be filled with everything
mihtam bilara kabia	in your hand it will be
Suerte man	Luck Charm you
naiwra wantkam takisa	today your power takes hold

Liwa waihwan	Mermaid enemy
Liwa waihwanka man	Mermaid enemy you
yula daiwira man	you dog killer
yula daiwra bri	bring on the dog killer
upla pliki sakisma	search for people and take them away
misbarka man	you hateful thing you
liwa puhknika nara	Mermaid medicine here
baikaika man	you counteractive potion
naiwa Praidi	today, Friday,
mai alkisna	this potion strikes you

MERMAID SICKNESS

Miskitu men and women contend that Mermaid, or liwa mairin, sickness is a broader category of illness that is associated with spirit molestation or spirit possession (Barrett 1992; García 1996a:123). Liwa sickness is usually diagnosed in individuals who have a nightly dream that an attractive person is making love to them—during the water spirit's nightly visits, the liwa "bothers," "molests," or "rapes" his or her victim. When the stricken person awakens, he or she commonly reports still being sweaty and aroused. The liwa sometimes leaves physical proof of lovemaking, such as bruises or red marks on the victim's body. Dennis (2004) contends that having liwa siknis (Mermaid sickness) indicates that the Mermaid is attracted to you and is a reflection of a person's sexual power. Men with liwa siknis may have pain in the groin area when urinating or have irregular secretions from the penis. This type of liwa sickness may be related to sexually transmitted disease. The Miskitu themselves also link this type of liwa sickness with the sexual domain. They believe that the liwa causes sickness in humans by entering the groin area from underneath the water when one is bathing or swimming in the rivers and lagoons.

Liwa mairin sickness has become synonymous with decompression sickness, or the bends, along the north coast of the Plátano Biosphere. When a diver has symptoms of liwa sickness, such as paralysis of the legs, the boat captains do not always take him directly to the nearest scuba-diving site or hospital with a decompression chamber; both Anthony's Key Resort in Roátan and the hospitals in Awas and La Ceiba have decompression chambers. Captains may simply drop off the injured diver on shore for treatment by local healers (suhkias) and plant specialists (*curanderos*), shirking their responsibilities to the injured diver. To a large extent, a syncretization of western and autochthonous systems of illness and healing has ensued in attempts to cure decompression or Mermaid sickness. As occurs in Bilwi–Puerto Cabezas, divers are treated in hospitals with decompression chambers and later seek out local healers.

When, as the intermediary between the human and supernatural world, the suhkia is called upon to cure the lobster diver, she or he attempts to exorcise the Mermaid's spirit, which has possessed his soul (*lilka*). The suhkia massages a sick diver's body with herbs, chants incantations or sings *canticos* (short songs), and dances to contact the other world. The suhkia also keeps the diver on a specific diet while being cured—he must avoid eating all seafood products and curly noodles, which suhkias claim resemble the Mermaid's long, blonde hair underwater. Meanwhile, the diver must adhere to a set of curing restrictions

FIGURE 37.
A Miskitu dance
troop in Bilwi
performing a skit
called "Liwa Mairin"
(PHOTO CREDIT:
Laura Herlihy)

known as *damni wan*, including not interacting with or seeing menstruating women, women or men who have recently had sex, or anyone who has viewed a dead person (i.e., gone to a velorio, or funeral). Often the suhkia does successfully exorcise the spirit of the Mermaid and cure (*rakaia* or *rawaia*) the diver.

During my fieldwork I saw a Miskitu dance troop in Bilwi–Puerto Cabezas, Nicaragua, perform a skit called "Liwa Mairin."[6] The main players included the Mermaid, the lobster diver, and the shaman. Through dance and gesture they acted out how the diver was possessed by the Mermaid and became ill. The suhkia cured the diver and gave him a tup, or amulet, to prevent the Mermaid from harming him in the future. Nevertheless, the Mermaid relentlessly pursued the diver with whom she had fallen in love and eventually beguiled him. In the end the diver willingly swam away to sea with the Mermaid and threw his amulet away, yanking it from around his own neck. Thereafter the diver was believed to have disappeared from this earth to live forever with the Mermaid in the other world beneath the sea.

Divers also believe they can make a deal or contract with the Mermaid by exchanging the life of a child for a big kill of lobsters (see also Jamieson 2009). They claim that the diver must first bring the Mermaid a pair of the child's underwear or a small garment, leaving it on a rock at sea. The garment represents the child's lilka, or soul, which the liwa wants to possess or abduct. According to local lore, by the time the diver returns to shore with the promised big kill of lobsters, this child (sometimes a stranger to the village) will have already died. This story repeatedly has been used to explain the sudden death of a small child in Kuri, especially if the deceased child's skin was marked by a rash or skin discoloration, symptoms associated with Mermaid sickness. Families often argue that a rival of the deceased child's father had a large kill at the same time that the child died. This is proof enough for some that the rival diver sold the child's soul to the Mermaid. A cycle of revenge killings through the use of poisons or hexes often results.

New systems of illness and healing have developed within the lobster industry, as revealed through the Mermaid. We have seen the relatively new diagnosis of liwa siknis as a disease that afflicts lobster divers who become greedy or the victims of divers who make deals with the ocean Mermaid, trading a human life for lobster and ultimately, cash. Jamieson (2009) calls the Miskitu people's contracts with Miskitu spirits and devils negative exchange relations, because the men ultimately lose more than they receive. Following Jamieson, while lobsters and money are renewable resources, human life is not. This demonstrates that a negative exchange principle, guided by the logic of market-based capitalism, now determines the relationship between Miskitu men and the main Miskitu spirit. This form of exchange with the Mermaid is exploitative of both divers and lobsters (Jamieson 2009). Together with chapter 6, my research here demonstrates that Miskitu men fear the sexuality of both human and supernatural women, like the beautiful but treacherous Mermaid.

Conclusion

Caribbean Vibrations

The Río Plátano Miskitu people's forty-year participation in the lobster economy has left an indelible imprint on their society. In the 1990s Miskitu communities were organized by matrifocal families and monetized relations between women and men, findings that have not previously been reported in the literature on the Miskitu. These findings, in addition to my research in chapter 1 regarding a present-day, "mixed" Miskitu socio-racial identity, contribute to the emerging understanding of the identity of the Honduran Miskitu people in the social scientific literature. My research demonstrates that the Honduran Miskitu people have many practices and identities similar to those of Afro-Caribbean societies (Bush 1990; Wekker 2006; Brennan 2004; Kempadoo 2009; Safa 1995; Gonzalez 1988; Smith 1996). This worthwhile contribution balances the plethora of research that focuses on the Nicaraguan Miskitu people as "Indian" warriors within the Latin American nation-state.

CENTRAL AMERICAN GENDER IDEOLOGIES

Robert C. West and John Augelli's *Middle America* is a classic textbook in cultural geography. Middle America refers to Mexico, Central America, and the

Caribbean. West and Augelli describe Central America by contrasting the Pacific highlands with the eastern Caribbean lowlands. Significantly, they explain that English-speaking black Protestants and indigenous peoples live in the remote rainforest and coastal regions of the Caribbean lowlands, contrasting that with the densely populated Pacific highlands, which historically have been home to the majority mestizo (Indian and Spanish), Spanish-speaking Catholic population.[1] West and Augelli argue that the Central American Caribbean lowlands are part of the circum-Caribbean culture area, which links the culture traits present on the Miskito Coast with the greater Caribbean.

In Mexico and Central America's Pacific highlands, patriarchal gender ideologies were firmly established in the colonial era. The law of "Patria Potestad" throughout Latin American colonies ensured men alone the right of personhood and legal adult status. Colonial law considered women the property of their fathers and, after marriage, of their husbands. Social institutions such as the Catholic Church reinforced patriarchal structures by organizing the clergy through nuclear families and recognizing male heads of household. The "honor-shame" code of behavior prevailed, in which a family's honor was defined by both social status and virtue. Men garnered honor by maintaining a firm economic hold over their household and control over their wife's and their daughters' sexuality. Behavioral norms for women dictated that they remain virgins until marriage, and once married they were forbidden to engage in acts of infidelity or to remarry after being widowed. Controlling women's sexuality was necessary to maintain the Spaniards' purity of blood (*limpieza de sangre*) and to justify patrilineal inheritance. Women's behaviors were also policed in the streets. As a woman in polite society, a lady (*doña*) was expected to surround herself with the trappings of domesticity and remain behind the protective walls of her home. Women who transgressed the prescribed social roles became sexual suspects who brought shame to their families and dishonor to men. Men, on the other hand, invested in *machista* ideology, in which seducing women and having many wives and children increased their perceived level of manhood in society (Gutmann 2003; Johnson and Lipsett-Rivera 1998; Lancaster 1991; Twinam 2001).[2]

The Spanish domination of colonial Central America did not extend to the Miskito Coast, and the region was spared many of the patriarchal ideologies that emanated from the Spanish culture of conquest, the social institution of the Catholic Church, and hegemonic colonial rule. Separated from the interior by a vast and spectacular tropical rainforest, the Miskito Coast was isolated and cut off from the department of Taguzgalpa, the eastern province of the Audiencia de Guatemala, during the colonial period (Offen 2002). The Miskito Coast remained out of reach of the long arm of Spanish control until 1860, when it was officially incorporated into the independent Honduran state. Catholicism did affect the more southern, riverine Moskitia settlements by way of *reducciones* in the early colonial period; however, the Catholic Church did not make further inroads into northern Moskitia due to the British presence and influence. Moravian missionaries did introduce patriarchal ideologies, yet the Moravian congregations on the north coast of the Plátano biosphere were not fully functioning until the middle of the twentieth century. Christianity first arrived on the Honduran coast in 1890, but Miskitu families were not missionized until the 1930s, when English-speaking German Protestant Moravians established churches in the north coast settlements of Brus Lakun, Cocobila, and Río Plátano (Tillman 2004; W. Marx 1980). Consequently, western patriarchal societal norms had relatively little influence on Honduran north coast settlements, especially when compared to New Spain, or what is today the Pacific coast of Central America and Mexico.

Gender and Globalization

Western values and monetized economies arrived during the early colonial era and have remained constant influences on the Miskito Coast (Hale 1994; Dennis 2004; Pineda 2006). The mixed Miskitu peoples (Afro-descendant, European, and indigenous) emerged as an ethnic group in the sixteenth century, when women began to marry foreign men and pass down Miskitu language and identity to their children in matrigroups. As residents of a British protectorate, the Miskitu people made economic and political alliances with the British but maintained indigenous cultural traditions and were not subject to enforced culture change through direct colonial rule. When the Honduran state reincorporated the Miskito Coast in 1860, the Honduran government's bureaucracy began to recognize male surnames and identify men as property owners and legitimate authorities, thus disregarding indigenous practices of inheritance and domestic organization. Interactions with both the state and the Protestant Moravian Church in the past 150 years have encouraged sexual segregation, a gendered division of labor, and a male-dominant gender ideology in Miskitu society. Male power, however, has been most blatantly solidified through a political economy in which employment opportunities have existed only for men.

Development studies in Latin America consistently find that poor and minority women suffer the most from economic globalization due to neoliberal governmental policies. This ethnography reveals the everyday ways in which Honduran indigenous women engage with contemporary globalization. Miskitu women negotiate their identities and status between the local discourse arising from their female-centered kinship groups and the more patriarchal discourses emanating from the Honduran state, westernized religions, and neoliberal economic models. My research shows, however, that women's oppression results not only from interactions with outside forces. Oppressive patriarchal ideologies revolving around perceptions of men as resource providers also arise at the local and regional level, discouraging women from entering the labor force.

Neoliberal economic models were established in the greater Caribbean in the early 1980s. Caribbeanist scholars of gender and globalization have documented women's successful entrance into the workforce (Yelvington 1995). Women reportedly have had more success than men in the workplace, due to the belief that Caribbean women are more financially responsible than men. Women are perceived to have developed leadership skills within their families as household heads (L. Herlihy 2010; Mohanty 2003; Mohammed 1986). Safa (2005) reports that female-headed households and matrifocality are increasing even in the more patriarchally structured Spanish Caribbean, due to the entrance of women garment workers into the workforce. Miskitu women have not entered the workforce as factory or farm workers, yet matrifocality clearly has developed in Miskitu society as a side effect of contemporary economic globalization.

Gender and globalization intersect on the Miskito Coast in paradoxical ways. Contradictory and competing discourses of gendered power exist in Kuri, a town financially supported by men but administered by women. Only men have access to steady work, as deepwater lobster divers. Women's desire for meat, money, and other store-bought goods that men provide reinforces the male-dominant political economy that operates in Honduran Moskitia. At the same time, though, the absence of men from their communities has led to a heightening of women's domestic power. Analysis suggests that in coastal Miskitu communities matriarchal structures exist alongside strong patriarchal norms (see also Cole 1991; Helms 1971; Sanday 2002).[3] Shanti Menon (1995) and Smith (1956, 1996) have recognized contradictory gender and power relations as central to matrifocal families.

Matrifocal domestic organization has taken hold in coastal Honduran Miskitu communities with the development of the lobster economy. My consideration of matrifocality builds on the work of other researchers in Nicaragua. Previous research in Nicaraguan Miskitu communities by García (1996a), Helms (1971), and Peter Espinoza (2006) reports matrilocality co-occurring with patrilineal kinship and descent. However, my research describes matrilocal residence patterns combining with mother-centered domestic groups and increasingly matrilineal descent to bolster women's status. The loss of the kiamp (patrilineal descent group) in Honduran Miskitu social organization, as discussed in chapter 3, offers a major point of departure for arguing the case of mother-centered domestic organization.

Gonzalez (1969, 1970, 1988) studied matrifocality among the Garífuna peoples in coastal Guatemala, to the west of Moskitia. She describes Garífuna "matrifocal units" as being composed of a senior woman—a single mother herself—living together with her unmarried daughters and children and, at times, some unmarried sons (Gonzalez 1970; see also Smith 1996; Tanner 1974:132). Single mothers in Garífuna domestic groups, then, continue to reside in their mother's home. Gonzalez (1970:1–12) also notes that senior women in Garífuna matrifocal units play the role of psychological head of the family. Similar to Garífuna practices, Creole families along the Central American Atlantic coast also live in multigenerational households where the senior woman serves as the family leader (CEIMM 2008:4). I found that nearly half of all Miskitu mothers in Kuri were single mothers but only a few continued to live in their mother's home (L. Herlihy 2006:47–48). Young Miskitu women more commonly move into their own household after having their first children. Individual Miskitu households do, however, tie into a larger matrilocal group under the control of a senior woman, or kuka. Thus Miskitu, Garífuna, and Creole families live in female-centered kinship groups in which senior women maintain ultimate authority. This suggests that a regional matrifocality exists on the Central American Caribbean coast.

The book also explores the ways in which commodified gender and sexual identities have intensified in Miskitu society during the development of the lobster economy. My research focuses on ethnolinguistic data related to buzo lawanka (men's lobster-diver songs) and praidi saihka (women's sexual magic incantations) as windows through which to view commodified gender and sexual identities. More descriptive ethnographic data on mairin mana (the exchange of cash for sex relations) and liwa mairin siknis (the bends, or

Mermaid sickness) provide additional examples of monetized gender identities. Central to my argument is that all of these manifestations of modern gender and sexual identities—buzo song lyrics, sexual magic, mairin mana, and Mermaid sickness—have taken their current shape within the lobster industry.

The songs demonstrate that being a man is now defined as being a rich and generous lobster diver. For men, music and songs function as a valve to express some of the conflictive emotions and demands that they deal with, primarily regarding their dangerous occupation and the dependence of the whole population on their financial contributions for survival. A diver's manhood has become linked to his potential as a wage earner, causing men to feel lonely at sea and insecure while back onshore, as they suspect that women welcome them back home only in order to access their money. Increasingly, women prefer to be in a position where they possess their husband's earning but their husband is physically absent from home. Some men claim that women will be when they die because their wife will receive a cash payment they die at sea. The ethnographic data and the broad spectrum of the lobster-diver songs reveal that men's bodies have been mercantilized within the lobster economy.

Women's sex magic incantations reveal that being a Plátano Miskitu woman today has to do with manipulating men into giving them their money. The data on sexual magic (praidi saihka) serve a double methodological purpose. Women's use of sexual magic also demonstrates their agentive capacities. Miskitu women, then, gain power and assets through capabilities learned in female-centered kinship groups. Coalitions of related women (mothers, daughters, and sisters) gain access to money through a variety of everyday and supernatural strategies. Miskitu women, then, have responded creatively and on their own terms to capitalist principles and the encroaching market economy.

CARIBBEAN CULTURAL PRACTICES

Melville Herskovits (1941) traces matrifocality in the Caribbean to matrilineal societies in Africa but also theorizes that mother-centered domestic organization was a successful way to deal with the plantation system, in which the slave trade commonly had separated men from their wives and children. He also notes that black women in the Caribbean have historically been not only the bearers of culture but also the main actors in the preservation of cultural traditions (Herskovits and Herskovits 1947, in Bush 1990:153). Differing with Herskovits, Smith (1956) argues that matrifocality was related more to class and race and the economically marginalized position of poor black families. Matrifocality, Smith contends, evolved in the Caribbean because men had worked as migrant wage-laborers since the mid-nineteenth century. As a result, he believes, women formed reciprocity and sharing networks and raised their children together without the daily presence of men.[4] Helms (1971:23–28) originally found that Miskitu women were the "conservative cultural core," maintaining autochthonous practices more than men did. Following Helms, my research finds that male absenteeism in Plátano Miskitu society has resulted in women maintaining Miskitu cultural identity, including kinship relations and obligations between families.

Researchers have documented other social features in Caribbean societies similar to those that I found in Kuri. Besides matrifocal domestic organization and women maintaining traditional culture (Gonzales 1988; Smith 1956, 1996; Safa 2005), researchers also have documented the commodification of identities within the labor force (Safa 2005; Yelvington 1995, 2001), transactional sex between women and men (Chevannes 2001; Kempadoo 2009), and women's use of magic potions and spells to improve their everyday lives (Bush 1990; Hurston 1990; Kerns 1997; McClaurin 1996). Additionally, supernatural female spirits like the Mermaid, or liwa mairin, have been reported among other Caribbean peoples. In Haiti the Soucouyant is an oversexed, night-flying witch-woman (Anatol 2000), and Ezili Frida, a Vodou goddess, is known as a beautiful but deadly sexual aggressor (K. Brown 1991). I argue for the overwhelming correspondence in socioeconomic and religious practices between Plátano Miskitu and Caribbean societies.

The Miskitu practice of sihka is part of broader Miskitu religious practices, known also known as maña negra in Spanish, black magic in English, or waukataya in Miskitu. Waukataya is similar to Caribbean religions such as Obeah, Vodou, Hoo Doo, and Santería, which have blended African with indigenous and westernized religious practices. These Caribbean religions lack a structured hierarchy, have family specialists who pass down religious knowledge (sometimes in a handwritten book but mostly through oral tradition, from person to person), and commonly have women as religious specialists who preserve spirituality within the family and community (see also Barrett 1992; K. Brown 1991; Bush 1990; Kerns 1997; McClaurin 1996).

Women throughout Caribbean societies who practice African-based religions such as Vodou, Obeah, and Santería act as supernatural healers, priestesses, and leaders of female-ancestor cults (Bush 1990). Kerns (1997) documents the power that Garífuna women maintain as religious leaders and conduits to matrilineal ancestor spirits (see also Wright 1995). Plátano Miskitu women similarly are central players in healing activities; most of the true shamans (*shukias*) along the coast (five out of seven) were women. These shamans are also responsible for rituals that make contact with ancestor spirits of the dead, such as Sihkru and Pura Yapti. More commonly, Miskitu grandmothers are both respected and feared by others for possessing the knowledge associated with sexual magic. Kukas pass down highly guarded secrets of praidi saihka to their daughters and granddaughters in the private domain of the matrigroup.[5] Given that the incantations and recipes vary widely, matrigroups become associated with certain types of sexual magic. Knowledge of sexual magic recipes and incantations has become a central component of Miskitu cultural identity and female power in coastal villages (Cunningham 2003; L. Herlihy 2005, 2006; see also Few 2002; Lewis 2003).

African-based Caribbean religions commonly utilize the conjure tradition of charms, spells, and potions, in which practitioners harness good supernatural forces for luck regarding love and money and also evil forces to cause harm to someone in vengeance or out of spitefulness. Zora Neal Hurston (1990) explores folk remedies in the Hoo Doo religion (also known as "root work" or African American folk magic) practiced in the American South (Florida and Louisiana). Similar to Miskitu sihka potions, Hoo Doo potions are made with plants and animal parts, bodily fluids such as menstrual blood, and colognes such as Agua de Florida. Also akin to Miskitu potions, Hoo Doo potions and spells can be used by women to cause men to fall in love with them and to give them goods and money, to make men forget about other their wife and other girlfriends, and to manipulate a man into abandoning his home forever (Hurston 1990:276).

Many scholars view African-based religions in the Caribbean as a form of resistance to slavery and colonial culture (see, for example, Bush 1990). However, I view Miskitu women's use of sihka potions as resistance to the impending globalized market economy and the male-dominant lobster economy. Ultimately, this book demonstrates that while geopolitically part of Latin America, the Miskito Coast is socially and economically situated within the circum-Caribbean culture area.

Afterword

THIS BOOK RESULTS FROM FIELD RESEARCH COMPLETED MAINLY IN 1997–1998 and 2001 in the Miskitu village of Kuri. Now, almost a decade later, I realize that the book describes a time that has passed on the Miskito Coast. I recently returned from Kuri, where I observed that everyday life has changed considerably for its residents. While Kuri still has no running water or electricity, the village has become even more involved with consumerism, and cell phones and digital media are common, creating a strange juxtaposition between local and global culture. Additionally, Miskitu men now live more dangerous lives. The lobster divers face increasing danger due to overexploitation of the lobster resource—they must dive deeper and deeper to find lobsters, which increases their risk of injury.

When the lobster industry began in the early 1970s, lobsters were plentiful and men extracted them by free diving (without air tanks). The men began using tanks in the 1980s and, as the lobster resource steadily declined, the divers have been forced to dive deeper, heightening the risk of decompression sickness. At the time of my field research in 1997–1998 men were descending to the dangerous depths of 100 feet or more to extract lobsters. In 2010, during a return visit to the coast, I found that the divers were forced to descend to around 150 feet of ocean depth in order to find lobsters. Divers' earnings were also decreasing because the price of lobster per pound had dropped. Divers claim that they harvest less lobster today due to the depletion of the lobster resource and because more competition exists on boats, as the number of divers per boat has doubled (to about fifty).

Cocaine (*labsta pihni*) and narco-trafficking activities also have entered the region. The divers purchase and use crack cocaine regularly, even on the lobster-diving boats, which heightens their chance of injury while diving. Purchasing the addictive substance also diminishes the divers' economic contribution to their household. Due to these health-related and social problems, along with resource depletion, the lobster-diving industry is scheduled to end in 2011. The Honduran government, working with the Global Fish Alliance, passed an initiative—the Ordenamiento Regional de la Pesqueria de la Langosta del Caribe (*Panulirus argus*) (Reglamento OSP-02–09), signed by the Honduran fisheries minister in May 2009—to ban spiny lobster-diving on the Miskito Coast as of June 1, 2011 (Lisa Jackson, personal communication, September 2010).[1] The lobster-diving economy has supported Miskitu families for the past forty years. What will happen to the Miskitu people of Honduras if no other enterprise replaces the faltering lobster industry is yet to be seen.

Notes

Introduction

1. A kindergarten school was built in honor of Siksto George, who died in 2003. It is the first school to be located in Kuri.
2. "Waikna apu" can, for example, refer to the social status of a widow, an unmarried woman, or a woman whose husband is away for a short time. "Apu" differs in degree from the Spanish term "no hay," which describes more of a temporary state (for example, "Sí tenemos, pero no hay").

Chapter One

1. While the British viewed the colonial Miskitu as being at least in part Indian, calling them "Zambos y Mosquitos" or "Zambos-Mosquitos," the Spanish emphasized their African ancestry, referring to all Miskitu speakers as Zambos.
2. In creating the Miskitu monarchy, the British attempted to make their presence on the Miskito Coast legal in the eyes of the Spanish and other European powers. Scholars disagree as to whether Miskitu kings were pawns used by the British or whether they had real authority (Helms 1986; Dennis and Olien 1984).
3. The Miskitu and Garífuna are both mixed Amerindian and African peoples that live on the Miskito Coast. However, the Miskitu are today thought of as being more Indian than the Garífuna, who are associated with African descent (Helms 1977; Wade 1997; Mollett 2006). Wade (1997:36) explains that social scientists have not fully explored the mixed-race identity of the Miskitu and Garífuna but rather have focused on the Miskitu "Indians" within the context of the Latin American nation-state and on the Garífuna as "blacks" in the African diaspora (see, e.g., England 2006).
4. Biosphere reserves are internationally recognized conservation regions that are dedicated to protecting the natural and cultural heritage of these regions for all humankind (Halffter 1985:15–18). UNESCO's program is responsible for the creation of three hundred biosphere reserves around the world. The Río Plátano Biosphere Reserve, a region administered by COHDEFOR, the Honduran forestry agency, was the first of five such reserves established in Central America.

5. When I asked Honduran Miskitu interviewees why the Nicaraguan Miskitu speakers were more "pure," they claimed that Nicaraguan Miskitu women and men had fewer physical features associated with blackness and that the Nicaraguan Miskitu dialect retained more English vocabulary than their own. In this case, the Honduran Miskitu consider their Nicaraguan kinsmen, with more Anglo physical features and linguistic traits, to be more "Indian" than themselves. This exemplifies a case where whiteness and British ethnicity are associated with indigeneity.

6. The indigenous organization Yatama, headed by Brooklyn Rivera (the "lider maximo" of the Miskitu people for the past twenty-five years), sponsors Sihkru Tara. The festival alternates between Brus Lakun, Honduras, and Bilwi, Nicaragua, and transports three busloads of people across the Río Coco (Wangki Awala) each year. Most participants from Honduras who participate in Puerto Cabezas/Bilwi hail from Puerto Lempira, Honduras.

7. The canal was recently extended to Brus Lakun and is part of a larger indigenous canal system that developed along the Miskitu Coast.

8. All currency conversions in this book use a rate of 13.8 lempiras to 1 U.S. dollar, the exchange rate used in 1998, at the time I did my fieldwork. Amounts are rounded to the nearest dollar.

Chapter Two

1. The linguistic data that I assembled consist of the recorded texts of two highly ritualized speech events used by Kuri men and women: buzo lawana (lobster-diver songs) and praidi saihka (sexual magic) incantations. Lobster-diver songs are songs that men sing about their lives as migrant wage-laborers (deepwater lobster divers), and sexual magic incantations are prayers that women recite when concocting supernatural remedies in order to manipulate the men's emotions. To gather and transcribe the buzo songs, I worked with two divers in their twenties, Wilintin Suarez and Eusebio Guevara; for the praidi saihka incantations, I employed one woman in her early sixties, doña Meri. All three of my informants were bilingual (Miskitu and Spanish), although doña Meri spoke considerably less Spanish than the men. All of the transcriptions and translations were completed in the field. I would first transcribe a text in Miskitu, then translate it to Spanish, and then again, to English. The texts presented are shortened versions of the songs and incantations.

2. "Tasbaya saihka" literally means the earth's medicine ("saihka" is the possessive construct of "sika"). Many ethnobotanists and medical anthropologists have studied the plants used in Miskitu tasbaya saihka and their medicinal properties (Barrett 1992, Dennis 1988; Fagoth, Gioanetta, and Silva 1998; García 1996a; House and Sánchez 1997), yet praidi saihka is a widespread but little documented part of Miskitu culture, and especially Miskitu women's culture.

3. Since the 1980s this style has become popular within the discipline and is now known as narrative anthropology or ethnographic fiction. Mary Pratt (1986) argues that this writing style was not accepted by the academy before the 1980s because it was seen as less scientific. She further argues that this way of writing became accepted by the academy and not perceived as weak and substandard only when male anthropologists with tenure adopted the style.

4. Plátano Miskitu women often wait a year or more to give their children names, for two reasons. The first is that many children die in the first year of life and so are not considered fully human until they have survived at least a year (see also Scheper-Hughes 1992). Also, Miskitu mothers prefer to give a child a unique name, one that no one else has along the coast. When North Americans or Northern Europeans arrived on the coast, mothers would bring their children to them and ask for a name. The visitors' suggestions of common first names were usually rejected, and they were often pushed to list off dozens and dozens of names, causing a fatigue to set in, which pushed visitors into the area of suspect suggestions. For example, children named Madona, Brusli, and Bilklintin (used as a first name) were present on the coast when I was there. Many mothers came to my house in search of lesser-known first names for their children—the names of all of my sisters and brothers, my high school girlfriends, and many of my former boyfriends saturate the north coast villages.

5. Haraway's (1988) concept of situated knowledges deals with the feminist ethnographic dilemma. Haraway contends that knowledge is always produced by an individual subject-actor who is located in a particular social and historical context.

6. New Orleans had the largest population of free people of color (*gens de couleur libre*) in the pre–Civil War United States and today still has a large population of Creoles—"mixed," or mulatto, descendants of French-speaking Europeans—who form part of the city's socially elite class that dominates the political and arts scene. The Creole population in New Orleans is not considered or called "black," and I do not refer to this segment of the African American population as those with whom I interacted as domestics or in the service industry. Indeed, the Creoles maintain quite a separate cultural and social space and do not readily interact with or intermarry whites or "blacks" in the city.

7. Carnival begins on King's Day, twelve days after Christmas, and rolls along through Fat Tuesday, the day before Lent begins.

8. Ethnographies written by women in the 1980s (D. Bell 1993; Shostak 1981) discussed women's roles and power in society but not always in relation to men. These female anthropologists seemed to champion personal and political causes by describing feminist utopias with high sisterly solidarity. Price's (1993) examination of menstruation huts in Maroon society, however, realistically portrayed women participants as independent but not as matriarchs having power meetings once a month.

Chapter Three

1. Patricia Mohammed (1986) earlier reported four characteristics of matrifocality commonly noted by researchers: an emphasis on women having high status; women being the main wage earners; women controlling the household economy; and situations in which male absenteeism caused the formation of female-headed households.

2. Building on Judith Butler's (2002) argument that western notions of kinship are inherently heterosexual, Blackwood deconstructs anthropology's heteronormative assumptions: that kinship is based on a man-woman marriage, a nuclear family, and a "Patriarchal Man" who is the main wage earner and head of household

(Blackwood 2005:8–10; see also Lamphere 2005). She believes that these views cause anthropologists to emphasize the fact that marriages are aberrant or weak in matrifocal societies, while ignoring the women's other forms of relatedness, such as partnerships. Blackwood succeeds in pointing out anthropological prejudices and reifies LGBTQ scholars who champion the cause of non-nuclear families (with no man-woman unit).

3. During interviews I also found that men were normally named as village and neighborhood founders because they had physically cleared the land. After being cleared, however, the land was passed down mainly through the female line. Many Plátano Miskitu husbands eventually purchased their own terrain and, in addition to the wife's inheritance, passed these lands down to their children. Bilateral inheritance of land increasingly predominates.

Disputes over land titling have occurred in the past twenty years. Only the wealthiest families have the resources to travel to the municipality (Brus Laguna) to obtain legal documentation of their landholdings. Some family members have contested such claims, saying that individual family members do not have private rights to communal family lands. These legitimate contestations remain unresolved in the legal arena, given the status of the lands as part of a biosphere reserve. Privatizing lands is becoming common practice, even though those who do it are considered tricky or thieves.

4. Many sisters lent their teenage daughters to their mothers and sisters in need, even from birth. Three of Kuka Denecela's daughters were the closest of sisters despite the fact that they had been raised in different houses.

5. Wekker (2006) reports that women in Surinam have several short relationships with various men, and even other women, who may temporarily become domestic and sexual partners. Wekker especially focuses on *mati*, same-sex friendships that often entail erotic satisfaction.

6. The Miskitu word "aisaia" means "to talk." But aisaia is also used as a euphemism for having sexual relations. Many Kuri women told me that their husbands beat them when they "talked" to other men. In Miskitu marriages violence often results when men are jealous and feel they cannot control their spouse's sexuality (CEIMM 2008). Women may fight back, which causes the violence to escalate. Sihka, or magic potions, are also believed to incite a divorce. Typically, a meddling relative or a vying partner is blamed for putting a *misbara*, or hate potion, on a man, causing him to desert his home and family.

7. Older residents of Kuri still understand the word "kiampka" (the suffix–ka is possessive) as used to refer to one's father's family, such as Ferrera kiampka. Younger ones, however, use the term "kiamp" (without the suffix) to refer to one's seasonal agricultural camp (this may come from "camp" in English; see also Dodds 2001). In the camp work is shared by members of the matrigroup. Dennis (2004:57) states that the word "kiamp" means plant root.

8. Anthropological theories of kinship and gender, beginning with M. Kay Martin and Barbara Voorhies (1975) and Ernestine Friedl (1975), build on the premise that women have higher status in societies with matrilocal residence and matrilineal descent than in societies characterized by patrilocality and patriliny. This theory specifically applies to horticulturally based societies like the Miskitu, where women participate in subsistence activities.

Chapter Four

1. Every item or service on the coast has a price, and conversations center on their current market price. When we first arrived in the Río Plátano region, we often felt antagonized by Miskitu individuals who asked the price of everything we owned, where we bought it, and if we would sell it. This seemed ridiculous at times, especially when they wanted to buy my husband's prescription eyeglasses. Many times locals aggressively took stock of our goods. As time went by, I realized that we should not interpret this as threatening or aggressive but as part of a culturally accepted mode of behavior, especially when encountering goods from afar.

2. When buzos return home with money, they expect to have a clean home, a cooked meal, and their wife and children washed and well-dressed. Likewise, buzo wives want to do everything in their power to ensure that they receive their husband's newly earned cash. Considering this, Kuri women were rarely caught off-guard by their husband's arrival—they usually received messages on shortwave radios from boat captains, communicated with other women whose husbands were on the same boat, and sighted their husbands' boats from the beach.

3. Rosali hardly ever used her flashlight to spotlight a person like a deer in the headlights; this was considered aggressive, rude behavior. I witnessed this only once, when a drunk came to Rosali's door in the middle of the night. Rosali slowly approached the door, jerked it open quickly, and shined the flashlight just above the man's eyes, on the forehead: "Dia want?" (What do you want?). Often Rosali used her flashlight to entertain her female friends at night. At first trailing behind them on the footpath, she would hustle to get to the beach ahead of them and then circle back. Dressed in black for invisibility, Rosali would stand close to them in silence, crack a joke, and then shine the light quickly on her own face to startle them.

Chapter Five

1. The north coast is one of the most important economic hubs of the Moskitia region. Men seasonally immigrate to the coast from nearby regions, such as Brus Lakun, Paulaya, Baltimore, and the upper Plátano and Patuca, to work on lobster-diving boats. The largest lobster industry thrives elsewhere along the Miskitu Coast of Honduras around the so-called Zona Recuperada (the territory closest to the Nicaraguan border). Lobster boats do not generally take divers from Garífuna settlements or from the Miskitu town of Brus Lakun, set back from the coast by a huge lagoon. The lobster business picks up again in Barra Patuca, just east of Brus, but some boats from the Patuca region have recently switched to the reserve's north coast. Their captains reportedly claimed that Plátano Miskitu workers had fewer problems than ones from the Patuca.

2. Other verses of "Awal tara wina" ("From the big river") discuss the theme of the difficulty of working alongside sharks. Although none have died from shark attacks, many divers have been bitten by sharks, barricudas, and other potentially harmful fish.

Awal tara wina	From the big river
warki pliskara ai bri wasata	They brought me to my place of
nahki daukamnaki	work how will I do it?

nahki daukamnaki	how will I do it?
nahki daukamnaki	how will I do it?
ilili manis na	there are a lot of sharks here
nahki daukamnaki	how will I do it?
ilili manis na	there are a lot of sharks here
nahki daukamnaki	how will I make it?

3. Dennis (2003) describes cocaine use in Miskitu villages.

4. This definition comes from *Merriam-Webster's Collegiate Dictionary*, 2002. Dennis (2004:142) also states, "Decompression sickness results from breathing compressed air, in which nitrogen is the major component, and then rising from the depths to the surface too rapidly."

5. The song was semiautobiographical, based on a true story. The woman named Minerva had been seen asleep in the tall grass, naked, in Kuri one morning and everyone had heard about it. That night, at my house, Eusebio spontaneously wrote "Minerva Mairin" while playing around on the guitar and singing. Many villagers laughed out loud when they heard the song playing from my jam box and would later congratulate Eusebio on his pretty and witty song.

6. His father, Modesto Morales, was a Miskitu elementary teacher and my first Miskitu-language tutor. Modesto Morales also was a promoter of traditional Miskitu song and dance and formed one of the first musical groups, Ecos de la Moskitia. Modesto brought groups of children to Tegucigalpa to perform in cultural events.

7. Lobster divers often consume large quantities of alcohol, which adds fuel to the proverbial fire between the sexes. Young divers sometimes get so drunk that they spend or lose all of their money in one night. They wake up broke, awaiting the next boat out to sea to earn more cash. These situations often involve a woman.

8. Canoe making has been both a historic and a modern-day Miskitu wage-earning activity, one for which the neighboring Tawahka people are today better known (McSweeney 2000).

Chapter Six

1. Plátano women claim that male divers under the spell of a magic potion give larger amounts of mairin mana after sexual relations.

2. A young woman still living in her mother's house may slip out during the night after hearing a diver give her a verbal signal from outside. She may leave through the window and, if caught by her mother, invent a reason or excuse for leaving the house at night; often girls claim that they had to go outside to defecate.

3. "Saihka" is the construct of the word "sihka" and means the medicine of some person, place, or thing.

4. Linguist Ken Hale (personal communication) believes the ancient form of the Miskitu word "sihka" is "ba sika." The nearby Tawahka people (who speak Tawahka Sumu, also a Macro-Chibchan, Misumalpan language) use the word "ba sika" to refer to medicine. Hale contends that the word "ba sika" is related to the Tawahka word "basni" (leaf).

5. A counteractive potion is called *klakaika* or *kangbaia* (*contra* in Spanish). Tup (charms or amulets) have the same counteractive effect. Some divers take medicines to protect themselves from other men—medicines that enhance their fighting abilities and physical strength. These sihkas are believed to prevent the divers from being killed during their frequent brawls back on shore. Two sihkas are often used in conjunction: *aiklabaia* ("fighting medicine"), which makes a man a better fighter, and *suapaihka*, (weakening medicine), which takes away the strength of his enemy.

6. During interviews the women did not report how much money they earned directly as a result of having used sexual magic. However, they did report the amount that men gave them as presents. It is understood, but never admitted, that women rely on potions to maximize these gifts. Thus the details of sexual magic and household income fall off the radar as secret information.

7. In her feminist ethnography Diane Bell (1993) notes that Australian aboriginal women use sexual magic to control mate selection, maintain marriages, and inherit land.

8. For more on Garífuna women's use of sexual magic, see Coehlo (1955), Gonzalez (1969), Kerns (1997), and Taylor (1951).

9. Lila Abu-Lughod's 1986 book, *Veiled Sentiments: Honor and Poetry in a Bedouin Society*, describes how counter-discourses function as anti-structure to the dominant ideology. Abu-Lughod demonstrates that, paradoxically, counter-discourses coexist with the dominant discourse. This seems to be the case with magic potions in Honduras.

10. Miskitu women choose to secretly contest the coastal gender ideology by never openly critiquing men; the secretive nature of women's speech practices illustrates their subordinate position to men (Menon 1995).

Chapter Seven

1. The coastal Miskitu claim that the liwa takes on human form in dreams and may even appear as a friend or person of the same sex. She does this in order to keep her identity a secret and trick her victim. Kuka Denecela insisted that the liwa is smart and appears in a physical form that will be pleasing and not threatening. She may look like a lover, a friend, or a stranger, but it is really the liwa in human disguise.

2. Ethnographic accounts by pirates of the period, such as A. O. Exquemelin ([1685] 1981), Raveneau De Lussan (1930), and others, report that they hid their vessels in the many inlets and lagoons on the Miskito Coast. Barrett (1992:347) believes "that the term Merry Maid derives from the English Mermaid, and has linguistic and mythic roots in Sirens of Greek Mythology. Identification of the Spanish sirens as Merry Maid and the occasional description of *Liwa Mairin* as having a woman's body with a fish's tail give evidence for this argument." Barrett's theory of the origin of the Merry Maid is interesting and plausible but should not be taken as fact, especially given that the water spirit is a broad culture pattern in South American Amazonian societies.

3. South American ethnographies of the Peruvian Amazon and the coastal Guyanas report the existence of water spirits, although not in mermaid form (M. Brown 1986:52). The water spirits in the Peruvian Amazon, like in Moskitia, are sexual beings and take people to live with them underwater a their spouses. Among the

Warao (Surinam Maroons) water spirits called *nabaro* were attracted to and abduct menstruating women to live with them as their wives under the water (Price 1993:xix).

4. The Pech, along with the Miskito, believed that a treacherous Mermaid dwelled underwater at the river's bend near Liwa Raya.

5. When any other liwa is mentioned, locals distinguish it by sex and race (usually indicated by skin color).

6. The Liwa Mairin skit is performed to the song "Saimani-Mani Wapanka Yabalka" (literally, Saimani-Mani's road walk). Saimani is the name of the young woman with whom the lobster diver is in love. She walks around for days looking for her boyfriend, to no avail. The diver cannot withstand the sexual and commercial power that the Mermaid holds over his soul. In the end he willingly leaves his beloved Saimani to live as the husband of the Mermaid in her lavish underworld home, complete with gold, motorboats, and neverending seafood resources.

Conclusion

1. West and Augelli (1989) further contrast the colonial economies of each region—plantations in the Caribbean lowlands versus haciendas in the Pacific highlands—and the social hierarchies, in which a Northern European–mulatto–black hierarchy defines the lowland Caribbean and Spaniard–mestizo–Indian social stratification reflects the Pacific highlands.

2. The globalization of western values and neoliberal economics has impacted and restructured patriarchal gender ideologies in Latin America today (Almeras 2001; Chant 2001). Most significantly, men's role as provider has come into question. Women have entered the industrial workforce and more informal economic sectors since neoliberal economic measures were established in Latin America in the late 1980s. Marriages more often end in separation and divorce due to conflicts over changing gender roles, and the percentage of female-headed households in Latin America has increased. Researchers in Mexico report that *campesino* and indigenous men cannot earn a living farming and frequently migrate to find work, leaving women behind to raise children, find work, and economically fend for themselves (Stephen 2007). Gender roles also transform for women who migrate with their husbands, as both spouses must work for the economic survival of the household and men learn to accomplish many domestic tasks. Yet Latin American men are still trying to maintain a hold on their domestic patriarchy (Connell 1995; Jackson 2001; Kimmel, Hearn, and Connell 2004).

3. "Matrifocal" should not be used interchangeably with the word "matriarchal." As we have seen, Miskitu men, like other men in postcolonial Caribbean societies, maintain their authority in society as the main wage earners. However, researchers should not shy away from using the term "matriarchal" when female-dominant ideologies clearly present themselves, such as in matrifocal societies (Sanday 2002).

4. Afro-Caribbean women often had children with several different men over their lifetime, yet they were not looked down upon or legally sanctioned for sexual promiscuity (Safa 1995; Wekker 2006).

5. "Saihka" is the construct of the word "sihka" and means the medicine of some person, place, or thing.

Afterword

1. The Global Fish Alliance (Alianza PESCA Global), or G-FISH, is a USAID-sponsored program that operates in cooperation with the Darden Restaurants corporation and the nonprofit AED (partnering with World Wildlife Fund and the Nature Conservancy) to address sustainable fisheries and aquaculture (Lisa Jackson, personal communication, August 2010).

Glossary

The plural of a noun in Miskitu is normally constructed by adding "nani" to the singular form. For example, "kuka nani" and "sihka nani" mean grandmothers and medicines, respectively (Salamanca 1988). Throughout the book, however, I form plurals by adding the English plural marker (-s) to Miskitu words: (e.g., kukas, sihkas). Note that the English plural marker is not part of the Miskitu word.

Below, "(S)" indicates a Spanish term.

advans: Advance payment that buzos receive prior to leaving for work on the lobster boats.

ai lihkan: A type of sihka used to attract, seduce, or garner resources from one particular man.

aisabe: Good-bye.

aisaia: To speak.

aisi sakaia: An oration chanted to a plant before extracting it from the ground.

aiklabaia: A type of sihka used to make a man a stronger, better fighter.

aksbil: Sea turtle.

albahuina: Slave; literally, slave meat.

amia tikaia: A type of sihka that erases one's memories of former relationships.

anti: Kinship term for one's mother's sister.

aouu: Yes.

apu: There is no/are none; in Spanish, "no hay."

barra: The sandbar or edge of a body of water. Often used in village names, such as Barra Plátano, the village at the edge of the Río Plátano (S).

bodega: Bar; usually a home, made from local materials, that sells beer and rum when available (S).

buzo: Deepwater lobster diver (S).

cacao: A plant that produces beans that are ground into chocolate (S).

canticos: Short songs (S).

caracol: Conch. A name used to refer to Islanders.

cayuco: A large, barrel-shaped canoe made to navigate the sea (S). More often called a "dori" in Miskito.

cayuquero: A canoeman who works alongside the lobster diver.

CES: An acronym for the police force that used to work in the Río Plátano region.

champa: Seasonal work camp upriver for agricultural and hunting activities.

cocal: Coconut plantation (S). The Miskito word for coconut is "kuku."

comanche: Assistant to the sacabuzo; responsible for making sure a certain number of divers leave for their boats on time.

comedor: A small restaurant; usually a woman serving food out of her kitchen (S).

curandera: A plant specialist; often works with a suhkia, like a nurse to a doctor (S).

dahn: An expression that means there is no more, the resource has been depleted, or it is over.

dama: Kinship term for grandfather or respected male elder.

damni wan: A set of restrictions that a sick person must follow in order to be healed. Mainly, a person with an illness must not see females who are menstruating, anyone who has recently seen a dead person, or those who have recently engaged in sexual relations. All would have negative effects on the healing process.

dawan: Owner; often this refers to supernatural entities that are the owners of resources: plant spirits are called the owners of the plants, God in Christian churches is called the owner of the Earth and the other world, and the liwa mairin (mermaid) in the traditional Miskito belief system is thought of as the owner of all resources from the waterways.

doña: A term of respect for a married woman (S).

dori: A round-bottom boat for sea travel.

fogón: A clay hearth (S).

guamiles: Plantation plots of crops, such as plantains, yuca, or orange trees (S).

guaro: Rum distilled locally (S).

hechiceria: Witchcraft (S).

hospedaje: A tourist house where visitors and ecotourists can reside (S).

huba sitan: An evil person (Satan).

huina: Cooked meat.

implikaia: To steal; often Miskito individuals talk bad about their own people, accusing them of thievery.

Indio: A term used to refer to Ladinos (S).

Indiyin: Indian.

ini minit: Any minute.

Ispael: Ladino.

kabura: Being on the coast.

kaiki was: See you later; a polite and informal way to say good-bye.

kaiura: Yucca.

kaiura ikaia: A type of sihka that takes away a man's virility; literally, to kill the yucca, a metaphor for the penis.

kapi: Coffee.

Karibi: A Garífuna individual or the Garífuna culture group.

kasao: Cashew fruit.

kiamp: The traditional patrilineal descent group symbolized by a common male surname; in coastal Honduran society "kiamp" is now used to refer to a matrigroup.

kiampka: Family agricultural lands with seasonal work camps; called "champas" in Spanish and "camps" in English.

kikalmuk: Kinship term for the eldest sister, often shortened to "kikal."

kirbaia: To go out walking around and socializing; "paseando" in Spanish.

klakaika: Counteractive potion that locals take to defend themselves against sihkas that others put on them; also called "kangbaia" (Miskitu) and "contra" (S).

klaura: Being upriver.

Kriul: Ethnic term of reference for a Creole or English-speaking black.

kuka: Kinship term for grandmother figure or respected female elder.

kuku dusa: Coconut tree.

kupia ikaia: A type of sihka that prevents men from being jealous of their wives.

kupia karna: To be brave.

kupia pihni: A good person.

kupia saura: A mean or greedy person.

kupia siksa: An evil, bad, or mean person.

kunin: A lie, an exaggeration, or gossip; also, "turi aisisa."

labsta: Lobster.

labsta pihni: Cocaine; literally, white lobster. This term is used for cocaine because, like lobster, it is a money-making industry in the region.

labsta saihka: A sihka used to enhance one's chances of killing lobsters.

lakra: Kinship term for someone of the opposite sex but the same generation.

lalah: Money.

lalah apu: An emphatic way of saying to have no money; i.e., flat broke.

lalah brisa: To be rich (literally, to have money).

lalah dusa: An expression used to refer to men with money; like the expression "money bags."

lamlat: Sister-in-law.

landin: The canal's bank, which villagers use as a natural dock for their canoes.

lapia: Ritualized kinship term for she or he who cuts the umbilical cord of a child during birth; also, "klua klakisa."

lapta: Hot or passionate.

lasa: Spirit.

lawana: Song.

lempira: The Honduran national currency (S).

leña: Pine wood (S).

lilia: Happy.

lilka: The soul of a person; also, a picture or photograph.

liwa: Supernatural water spirits with different genders and races. The most common is the liwa mairin, or the Mermaid; also, "li dawanka" (creator and owner of all bodies of water and water life, including flora and fauna).

liwa mairin: The Mermaid.

liwa siknis: A variety of illnesses that the water spirits cause; most significantly, the bends (decompression sickness) in divers.

luhpia: Kinship term meaning child.

madrina: Christian godmother. In Miskito society, madrinas call the parents of the child "co-madre" and "co-padre," as in the Spanish-speaking world.

mahbra: Egg; also used as a euphemism for testicles.

maia: Spouse; defined as those who live together and usually have children.

maia prukaia: To yell at or hit one's spouse.

mairin: Woman.

mairin mana: An exchange of cash for sexual relations; society members define this commodification of affection not as prostitution but as a gift or present.

maisaia: Brother-in-law (from a woman's perspective).

mama tara: Another term for grandmother.

maña negra: Witchcraft (S).

marinero: Sailor; a position on the lobster boats that requires more education than the buzos have; typically marineros have to read the boat's instruments that direct its trajectory (such as a compass) (S).

meriki: An ethnic term of reference for a North American or northern European.

mestizo: Spanish speakers of Indian and Spanish descent (S).

millionario: Anyone having a moderate amount of wealth (S).

min: Mean spirited; used with the term "uba," as in "uba min" (really mean). Locals use the term for divers who do not buy them presents at the store.

misbara: A sihka that is used as a hate potion.

mochilas: Backpacks; buzos carry them to sea with all the belongings they will have for two weeks on the boat (S).

monte: Mountain or forest (S).

Moreno: A term used to refer to Garífuna people.

muihki: Kinship term of reference for someone of the same sex and same generation; thus cousins and siblings of the same sex are called "muihki." A half sibling is also called "muihki." Locals use the informal kinship term "muihki muihki" to refer to a sibling of the same sex from the same parents.

mulato: Someone of mixed European and African ancestry.

Musti: Ethnic term of reference for a Bay Islander.

mustro: A type of fish.

nance: A yellow fruit that looks like a berry (S).

nari: Spicy; used to describe food and also to refer to someone who is highly sexual and passionate.

Negro: Disrespectful ethnic term of reference for a Creole.

Nikru: A derogatory term used to refer to Afro-descendant people in the region.

pain: Fine.

palanca: A pole used to push a canoe upriver (S).

pana: Friend.

pauni: Red.

Paya: A term of reference for a Pech person.

piarka: Widow.

pihni: White.

pipante: A flat-bottomed river canoe (S); sometimes called "pitpan" in Miskito.

plaisni: Adoring kinship term for the youngest child; "seca leche" in Spanish.

plátanos: Bananas (S).

platu: A small species of banana grown locally.

plunki: An assistant to the cook on the lobster boats.

praidi saihka: A type of sihka, mainly made on Friday, that is used to control relationships and feelings. Women originally used praidi saihka potions for love but now use them mainly to garner resources from the lobster divers.

praut: Proud or self-righteous.

prisant: A gift; usually refers to the gift of money from a diver.

puhbaia: To blow upon; a method used in healing.

rakaia: To heal or cure.

ras awala: Río Plátano.

rintin: Secondhand clothes sold in the Kuri region.

ritskira: Very rich.

rum diaia: To drink rum.

sacabuzo: An employee of the boat captain who hires local men as divers (S).

sadi: Sad; used synonymously with "lala apu."

saura: Bad or ugly.

sihka: Any medicine used to heal emotional, spiritual, or physical illness, usually made with plants.

sihka saura: Supernatural medicine used to hurt, make sick, or kill others; "maña negra" (black magic) in Spanish.

slabla: Stingy.

stand-bai: A type of sihka used to coerce someone of the opposite sex into being attentive to one's every personal need.

suapaihka: A type of sihka that takes away the strength of one's enemy in battle. Divers use suapaihka to help them in fights that develop after they have returned to shore.

suhkia: A spiritual or supernatural healer.

Sumu: Ethnic term of reference for a Tawahka Sumu individual or the entire culture group.

tahti: Kinship term for mother's brother (see "tuban").

tambako: Christmas celebrations, including nighttime gatherings with dancing, singing, and guitar and drum playing. Tambako typically begins a few months before Christmas and lasts through New Year's Day.

tasbaya saihka: Natural medicine.

tasbaya taihka: Ritualized kinship term (literally, family of the land). The Miskito create a fictive kinship with non-family members who live in their village.

taya: A word that refers to family and skin.

taya pauni: Red skin.

taya pihni: White skin.

taya siksa: Black skin; also, "karibi" or "uba siksa" (too black).

tepesquintle: *Agouti paca* or *Cuniculus paca*, a large rodent, similar to a nutria.

tiara: An adolescent girl.

tilba: A tapir, a huge animal with an elephant-like trunk and a horse-like body native to Central and South American rainforests.

tingki: Thank you; "tingki pali" means "thanks a lot."

tingkikas: Ungrateful.

triswaia: To flirt.

trucha: Store.

tuban: Kinship term for a man's sister's son; corresponds with the kinship term "tahti" (mother's brother). The tuban-tahti (mother's son and mother's brother) kinship relationship is a special one between a boy and his mother's brother, who often supervises his entrance into manhood. These respectful kinship terms are often adopted as terms of reference by diver-canoeman teams, regardless of their actual relationship.

tuktan: Child.

tuktan mana: Money paid to a woman by a man to help feed her children.

tuk-tuk: A dugout canoe with an outboard motor, usually with little horsepower.

tup: A charm or amulet, usually used as a counteractive remedy to defend oneself against a sihka that another person may put on you. Divers use anti-liwa tup so that the Mermaid will not give them the bends.

twi: The savanna; also commonly called the "llano" in Spanish.

umpira: Destitute, poor, or pathetic.

upan: Raw meat.

upla: Person or people.

upla saura: Bad people to be avoided at all times.

upla wal aisaia apia: Snobbish people; literally, those who do not talk with others.

urkira: Prostitute.

utla: House.

vagando: Drifting, loitering, or roaming around, usually being up to no good (S).

verano: Dry season (January–June) (S); "mani tain" or "lapta mani" in Miskito.

veda: A four-month moratorium on lobster diving, from mid-April to mid-August (S).

velorio: A wake.

wabul: A traditional food made from mashed plantains and coconut water.

wahma: An adolescent male or young man.

waikna: A man or human being.

waikna apu: Without men.

waikna laikaia: To like men; often used with the word "uba" (meaning too much or a lot), as in "uba waikna laik" (to be boy crazy and promiscuous).

waikna saihka: Another term for praidi saihka; literally, man medicine.

wanina: Jealous.

wauwisa: A sihka that summons a person from afar to return home immediately.

waukataya: Black magic.

winsdi saihka: Another term for praidi saihka; literally, Wednesday medicine.

yabakaia: An oration chanted to a plant that includes an element of ritualized blowing.

yamni kaikan: Love; also used as the name of a type of sihka that makes all living things like you, including elders, children, and even animals.

yang: I (first-person pronoun in Miskito).

yapti: Kinship term used for mother; "mama" is also used. Often, "mama" and "yapti" are extended to one's aunts on one's mother's side.

yaura: A starchy tuber plant; "yuca" in Spanish.

yumuh: An oration chanted to a plant that uses more complicated ingredients and is more prayer-oriented than other orations.

Zambo: A derogatory term used to refer to the Miskitu people (S).

Bibliography

Abu-Lughod, Lila
  1986. *Veiled Sentiments: Honor and Poetry in a Bedouin Society.* Berkeley: University of California Press.
  1990. Can There Be a Feminist Ethnography? *Women and Performance: A Journal of Feminist Theory* 5(1):7–27.

Adams, Rachel, and David Savran, eds.
  2002. *The Masculinities Studies Reader.* Malden, MA: Blackwell.

Adams, Richard N.
  1981. The Sandinistas and the Indians: The "Problem" of Indians in Nicaragua. *Caribbean Review* 10(1):23–25.

Almeras, Diane
  2001. Equitable Social Practices and Masculine Personal History: A Santiago Study. In *Men at Work.* C. Jackson, ed. Pp. 139–56. London: Frank Cass.

Anatol, Giselle
  2000. Transforming the Skin-Shedding Soucouyant: Using Folklore to Reclaim Female Agency in Caribbean Literature. *Small Axe* 7:44–59.

Anderson, Mark
  1997. The Significance of Blackness: Representations of Garífuna in St. Vincent and Central America, 1700–1900. *Transforming Anthropology* 6(1–2):22–35.
  2001. Does Racism Exist in Honduras?: Mestizo Stereotypes and Garífuna Discourses. *Mesoamérica* 42:135–63.

Antonio, C., M. Antonio, E. M. Blanco, M. Cunningham, M. Ingram, M. McClean, S. Miguel, and C. Poveda
  2006. Proyecto Albuergue. Propuesta de proyecto para un albergue de Mujeres, elaborado por Myrna Cunningham de CADPI con la colaboración de la red de mujeres contra la violencia. Bilwi, Nicaragua: RAAN.

Bakewell, Liza
  2010. *Madre: Perilous Journeys with a Spanish Noun.* New York: W. W. Norton.

Barrett, Bruce P.

    1992. The Syringe and the Rooster Dance: Medical Anthropology on Nicaragua's Atlantic Coast. PhD dissertation, University of Wisconsin, Madison.

Behar, Ruth

    1987. Sex and Sin, Witchcraft and the Devil in Late-Colonial Mexico. *American Ethnologist* 14:35–55.

    1993. *Translated Woman: Crossing the Border with Esperanza's Story.* Boston: Beacon.

Behar, Ruth, and Deborah A. Gordon, eds.

    1995. *Women Writing Culture.* Berkeley: University of California Press.

Bell, Charles Napier

    1899. *Tangweera: Life and Adventures Among Gentle Savages.* London: Edward Arnold.

Bell, Diane

    1993. *Daughters of the Dreaming.* Minneapolis: University of Minnesota Press.

Blackwood, Evelyn

    2000. *Webs of Power: Women, Kin, and Community in a Sumatran Village.* Lanham, MD: Rowman and Littlefield.

    2005. Wedding Bell Blues: Marriage, Missing Men, and Matrifocal Follies. *American Ethnologist* 32(1): 3–19.

Boas, Franz

    1981. *Kwakiutl Ethnography.* 3rd edition. Helen Codere, ed. Chicago: University of Chicago Press.

Bonner, Donna M.

    1999. Beauty, Propriety and Status in a Former British Colony: European Aesthetic Theory and Social Distinctions Based upon Racial "Appearances" in Dangriga, Belize. *Social Analysis* 43(1):119–40.

Bourgois Philippe

    1981. Class, Ethnicity, and the State Among the Miskitu Amerindians of Northeastern Nicaragua. *Latin American Perspectives* 8(2):23–29.

Brennan, Denise

    2004. *What's Love Got to Do with It?: Transnational Desire and Sex Tourism in the Dominican Republic.* Durham, NC: Duke University Press.

Brettell, Caroline B.

    1986. *Men Who Migrate, Women Who Wait: Population and History in a Portuguese Parish.* Princeton, NJ: Princeton University Press.

Brogger, Jan, and David Gilmore

    1997. The Matrifocal Family in Iberia: Spain and Portugal Compared. *Ethnology* 36(1):13–30.

Brondo, Keri Vacanti

    2010. When Mestizo Becomes (Like) Indio . . . or Is It Garífuna?: Multicultural Rights and "Making Place" on Honduras' North Coast. *Journal of Latin American and Caribbean Anthropology* 15(1):170–94.

Brown, Karen McCarthy
  1991. *Mama Lola: A Vodou Priest in Brooklyn.* Berkeley: University of California
          Press.
Brown, Michael
  1986. *Tsewa's Gift: Magic and Meaning in an Amazonian Society.* Washington,
          D.C.: Smithsonian Institution Press.
  1996. On Resisting Resistance. *American Anthropologist* 98(4):729–49.
Bush, Barbara
  1990. *Slave Women in Caribbean Society, 1650–1838.* Bloomington: Indiana
          University Press.
Butler, Judith
  2002. Is Kinship Always Already Heterosexual? *Differences* 13(1):14–44.
CEIMM (Centro de Estudios e Información de la Mujer Mulitétnica)
  2008. Diagnóstico de género en las Regiones Autónomas de la Costa Caribe.
          Serie Cuadernos de Género para Nicaragua, 3. Managua, Nicaragua:
          Banco Mundial y Banco Interamericano de Desarrollo.
Chant, Sylvia
  2001. Men in Crisis? Reflections on Masculinities, Work, and Family in Northwest
          Costa Rica. In *Men at Work.* Cecile Jackson, ed. Pp. 199–218. London: Frank
          Cass.
Chevannes, Barry
  2001. *Learning to Be a Man: Culture, Socialization, and Gender Identity in Five
          Caribbean Communities.* Mona, Jamaica: University of the West Indies Press.
Clifford, James
  1986. On Ethnographic Allegory. In *Writing Culture: The Poetics and Politics
          of Ethnography.* James Clifford and George E. Marcus, eds. Pp. 98–121.
          Berkeley: University of California Press.
Coehlo, Roy
  1955. The Black Carib of Honduras: A Study in Acculturation. PhD dissertation,
          Northwestern University.
Cole, Sally
  1991. *Women of the Praia: Works and Lives in a Portuguese Coastal Community.*
          Princeton, NJ: Princeton University Press.
Connell, Robert W.
  1995. *Masculinities.* Berkeley: University of California Press.
Conzemius, Eduard
  1932. Ethnographic Survey of the Miskitu and Sumu Indians of Honduras and
          Nicaragua. Smithsonian Institution. Bureau of American Ethnology. Bulletin
          106. Washington, D.C.: U.S. Government Printing Office.
Cook, H. B. K.
  1992. Matrifocality and Female Aggression in Margariteño Society. In *Of Mice
          and Women: Aspects of Female Aggression.* K. Bjorkqvist and P. Nimela, eds.
          Pp. 149–62. San Diego: Academic.

Cunningham, Myrna Kain
  2003. Indigenous women and International Law. MADRE: An International
    Women's Human Rights Organization. http://www.madre.org/.
Davidson, William V.
  1976. Black Carib (Garífuna) Habitats in Central America. In *Frontier Adaptations
    in Lower Central America*. M. Helms and F. Loveland, eds. Pp. 86–94.
    Philadelphia: Institute for the Study of Human Issues.
De Lussan, Raveneau
  1930. *Buccaneer of the Spanish Main and Early French Filibuster of the Pacific*.
    Marguerite Eyer Wilbur, trans. Cleveland: Arthur C. Clark.
Dennis, Philip A.
  1981. Costeños and the Revolution in Nicaragua. *Journal of Interamerican Studies
    and Word Affairs* 23(3):271–96.
  1988. Herbal Medicine Among the Miskito of Eastern Nicaragua. *Economic
    Botany* 42(1):16–28.
  2003. Cocaine in Miskitu Villages. *Ethnology* 42(2):161–72.
  2004. *The Miskitu People of Awastara*. Austin: University of Texas Press.
Dennis, Philip A., and Michael D. Olien
  1984. Kingship Among the Miskito. *American Ethnologist* 11:718–37.
Diskin, Martin
  1991. Ethnic Discourse and the Challenge to Anthropology: The Nicaraguan Case.
    In *Nation-States and Indians in Latin America*. Greg Urban and Joel Sherzer,
    eds. Pp. 156–80. Austin: University of Texas Press.
Dodds, David
  1998. Lobster in the Rain Forest: The Political Ecology of Miskitu Wage Labor and
    Agricultural Deforestation. *Journal of Political Ecology* 5:83–108.
  2001. The Miskito of Honduras and Nicaragua. In *Endangered Peoples of Latin
    America: Struggles to Survive and Thrive*. Susan Stonich, ed. Pp. 87–99.
    Westport, CT: Greenwood.
England, Sarah
  2006. *Afro Central Americans in New York City: Garífuna Tales of Transnational
    Movements in Racialized Space*. Gainesville: University Press of Florida.
Exquemelin, A. O.
  [1685] *The Buccaneers of America*. Santo Domingo, Dominican Republic:
  1981. Corripio.
Fagoth, Ana Rosa, Fulvio Gioanetta, and Adán Silva
  1998. *Wan kaina kulkaia: Armonizando con nuestro entorno*. Managua, Nicaragua:
    Imprimatur Artes Gráficas.
Falla, Ricardo
  1982. El problema de los Miskitos en Nicaragua. *Estudios Centroamericanos*
    401:193–200.
Few, Martha
  2002. *Women Who Live Evil Lives: Gender, Religion, and the Politics of Power in
    Colonial Guatemala*. Austin: University of Texas Press.

Figueroa, J. Peter

    2008. The HIV Epidemic in the Caribbean: Meeting the Challenges of Achieving Universal Access to Prevention, Treatment, and Care. *West Indian Medical Journal* 57(3):195–203.

Floyd, Troy S.

    1967. *The Anglo-Spanish Struggle for Mosquitia.* Albuquerque: University of New Mexico Press.

Fonseca, Claudia.

    2001. Philanderers, Cuckolds, and Wily Women: A Reexamination of Gender Relations in a Brazilian Working-Class Neighborhood. *Men and Masculinities* 3:261–77.

Foucault, Michel

    1980. *Power/Knowledge: Selected Interviews and Other Writings, 1972–1977.* Colin Gordon, ed. New York: Vintage.

Friedl, Ernestine

    1975. *Women and Men: An Anthropologist's View.* New York: Holt, Rinehart and Winston.

Gal, Susan

    1991. Between Speech and Silence: The Problematics of Research on Language and Gender. In *Gender at the Crossroad of Knowledge: Feminist Anthropology in the Postmodern Era.* Micaela di Leonardo, ed. Pp. 175–203. Berkeley: University of California Press.

García, Claudia

    1996a. *The Making of the Miskitu People of Nicaragua: The Social Construction of Ethnic Identity.* Acta Universitatis Upsaliensis, Studia Sociologica Upsaliensia, 41. Uppsala, Sweden: Uppsala University.

    1996b. Qué implica ser madre en Asang, Río Coco. *Wani: Revista del Caribe Nicaragüeñse* (June–September):13–23.

Gilmore, David D.

    1991. *Manhood in the Making.* New Haven, CT: Yale University Press.

Goldstein, Donna M.

    2003. *Laughter Out of Place: Race, Class, Violence, and Sexuality in a Rio Shantytown.* Berkeley: University of California Press.

Gonzalez, Nancie

    1969. *Black Carib Household Structure.* Seattle: University of Washington Press.

    1970. Towards a Definition of Matrifocality. In *Afro-American Anthropology: Problems in Theory and Method.* N. Whitten Jr. and J. Szwed, eds. Pp. 231–43. New York: Free Press.

    1988. *Sojourners of the Caribbean: Ethnogenesis and Ethnohistory of the Garifuna.* Urbana: University of Illinois Press.

Gordon, Edmund T.

    1998. *Disparate Diasporas: Identity and Politics in an African-Nicaraguan Community.* Austin: University of Texas Press.

Gregor, Thomas

    1985. *Anxious Pleasures: The Sexual Lives of an Amazon People.* Chicago: University of Chicago Press.

Gutmann, Matthew C., ed.

    2003. *Changing Men and Masculinities in Latin America.* Durham, NC: Duke University Press.

Hale, Charles

    1987a. Institutional Struggle, Conflict and Reconciliation: Miskitu Indians and the Nicaraguan State (1979–1985). In *Ethnic Groups and the Nation State: The Case of the Atlantic Coast in Nicaragua.* CIDCA, Development Study Unit, eds. Pp. 101–28. Stockholm, Sweden: University of Stockholm.

    1987b. Inter-Ethnic Relations and Class Structure in Nicaragua's Atlantic Coast: An Historical Overview. In *Ethnic Groups and the Nation State: The Case of the Atlantic Coast in Nicaragua.* CIDCA, Development Study Unit, eds. Pp. 33–57. Stockholm, Sweden: University of Stockholm.

    1994. *Resistance and Contradiction: Miskitu Indians and the Nicaraguan State, 1894–1987.* Stanford, CA: Stanford University Press.

    1997. The Cultural Politics of Identity in Latin America. *Annual Review of Anthropology* 26:567–90.

Halffter, Gonzalo

    1985. Biosphere Reserves: Conservation of Nature for Man. *Parks* 10(3):15–18.

Haraway, Donna

    1988. Situated Knowledges: The Science Question in Feminism and the Privilege of the Partial Perspective. *Feminist Studies* 14(3):575–99.

    2005. Situated Knowledges: The Science Question in Feminism and the Privilege of the Partial Perspective. *Feminist Studies* 14(3):575–99.

Helms, Mary W.

    1969. The Purchase Society. *Anthropological Quarterly* 42(4):325–42.

    1970. Matrilocality, Social Structure and Culture Contact: Three Case Studies. *Southwestern Journal of Anthropology* 26:197–212.

    1971. *Asang: Adaptations to Culture Contact in a Miskito Community.* Gainesville: University Press of Florida.

    1976. Introduction. In *Frontier Adaptations in Lower Central America.* Mary W. Helms and Frank G. Loveland, eds. Pp.2–15. Philadelphia: Institute for the Study of Human Issues.

    1977. Negro or Indian? The Changing Identity of a Frontier Population. In *Old Roots in New Lands: Historical and Anthropological Perspectives on Black Experiences in the Americas.* Ann Pescatello, ed. Pp. 157–72.Westport, CT: Greenwood.

    1986. Of Kings and Context: Ethnohistorical Interpretations of Miskito Political Structure and Function. *American Ethnologist* 13:506–23.

    1993. *Craft and the Kingly Ideal: Art, Trade, and Power.* Austin: University of Texas Press.

Herdt, Gilbert H.

    1982. Fetish and Fantasy in Sambia Initiation. In *Rituals of Manhood.* Gilbert H. Herdt, ed. Pp. 44–98. Berkeley: University of California Press.

Herlihy, Laura Hobson
    2002. Miskitu Identity in the Río Plátano Biosphere Reserve, Honduras. *Indigenous Nations Studies Journal* 3(2):3–20.
    2005. Indigenous Masculinities in the Global Lobster Economy. *Southern Anthropologist* 31(1–2):35–52.
    2006. Sexual Magic and Money: Miskitu Women's Strategies in Northern Honduras. *Ethnology* 45(2):143–59.
    2007. Matrifocality and Women's Power on the Miskito Coast. *Ethnology* 46(2):133–50.
    2008. Neither Black nor Indian: The Discourse of Miskitu Racial Identity in Honduras. *Geoscience and Man* 40:129–44.
    2011. Rising Up? Indigenous and Afro-Descendant Women's Political Leadership in the RAAN. In *National Integration and Contested Autonomy: The Caribbean Coast of Nicaragua.* Luciano Baracco, ed. Pp. 221–42. New York: Algora.

Herlihy, Peter H.
    1993. Securing a Homeland: The Tawahka Sumu of Mosquitia's Rain Forest. In *State of the Peoples: A Global Human Rights Report on Societies in Danger.* Marc S. Miller, ed. Pp. 54–62. Boston: Beacon.
    2001. Indigenous and Ladino Peoples of the Río Plátano Biosphere Reserve, Honduras. In *Endangered Peoples of Latin America: Struggles to Survive and Thrive.* Susan Stonich, ed. Pp. 101–20. Westport, CT: Greenwood.

Herlihy, Peter H., and Laura Hobson Herlihy.
    1991. La herencia cultural de La Reserva de la Biosfera del Río Plátano: Un area de confluencias étnicas en La Mosquitia. In *Herencia de nuestro pasado: La Reserva de La Biosfera Río Plátano.* Vincente Murphy, ed. Pp. 9–15. Tegucigalpa, Honduras: ROCAP (USAID), Fundo Mundial para La Naturaleza (WWF), COHDEFOR, AID.

Herskovits, Melville J.
    1941. *The Myth of the Negro Past.* New York: Harper and Brothers.

Holm, John
    1978. The Creole English of Nicaragua's Atlantic Coast: Its Sociolinguistic History and a Comparative Study of Its Lexicon and Syntax. PhD thesis, University College, University of London.

House, Paul, and Indalesio Sánchez
    1997. *Mayangna panan basni / Plantas medicinales del pueblo Tawahka.* London: Natural History Museum.

Hurston, Zora Neal
    1990. *Mules and Men.* New York: Harper.

Jackson, Cecile
    2001. *Men at Work: Labour, Masculinities, Development.* London: Frank Cass.

Jamieson, Mark
    2000. It's Shame That Makes Men and Women Enemies: The Politics of Intimacy Among the Miskitu of Kakabila. *Journal of the Royal Anthropological Institute* 6(2):311–24.
    2001. Masks and Madness: Ritual Expressions of the Transition to Adulthood Among Miskitu Adolescents. *Social Anthropology* 9:257–72.

2009. Contracts with Satan: Relations with "Sprit Owners" and Apprehensions of the Economy Among the Coastal Miskitu of Nicaragua. *Durham Anthropology Journal* 16(2):44–53.

Johnson, Lyman L., and Sonya Lipsett-Rivera
1998. *The Faces of Honor: Sex, Shame, and Violence in Colonial Latin America.* Albuquerque: University of New Mexico Press.

Kempadoo, Kamala
2003. *Sexing the Caribbean: Gender, Race, and Sexual Labor.* New York: Routledge.
2009. Caribbean Sexuality: Mapping the Field. *Caribbean Review of Gender Studies* 3:1–24.

Kempadoo, Kamala, Jyoti Sanghera, and Bandana Pattanaik, eds.
2005. *Trafficking and Prostitution Reconsidered: New Perspectives on Migration, Sex Work, and Human Rights.* Boulder, CO: Paradigm.

Kerns, Virginia
1997. *Women and the Ancestors: Black Carib Kinship and Ritual.* 2nd edition. Urbana: University of Illinois Press.

Kimblad, Christopher
2001. *Gift and Exchange in the Reciprocal Regime of the Miskito on the Atlantic Coast of Nicaragua, Twentieth Century.* Dissertations in Sociology 44. Lund, Sweden: Lund University.
2010. *Gift and Exchange Among the Miskitu on the Atlantic Coast, Nicaragua: A Historical-Comparative Study on Cultural Change, 20th Century.* Saarbrücken, Germany: Lambert Academic.

Kimmel, Michael S, Jeff Hearn, and Robert W. Connell, eds.
2004. *Handbook of Studies on Men and Masculinities.* London: Sage.

Knauft, Bruce M.
1996. *Genealogies for the Present in Cultural Anthropology.* New York: Routledge.

Laird, Larry
1970. Origins of the Reincorporation of the Miskito Coast. MA thesis, University of Kansas.

Lamphere, Louise
2005. Replacing Heteronormative Views of Kinship and Marriage. *American Ethnologist* 32(1):34–36.

Lancaster, Roger
1991. Life Is Hard: Machismo, Danger, and the Intimacy of Power in Nicaragua. Berkeley: University of California Press.

Lewis, Laura A.
2003. *Hall of Mirrors: Power, Witchcraft, and Caste in Colonial Mexico.* Durham, NC: Duke University Press.

Malinowski, Bronislaw
1984. *Argonauts of the Western Pacific.* Prospect Heights, IL: Waveland.

Marcus, George, and Michael J. Fischer
1986. *Anthropology as Cultural Critique: An Experimental Moment in the Human Sciences.* Chicago: University of Chicago Press.

Martin, M. Kay, and Barbara Voorhies

    1975. *Female of the Species*. New York: Columbia University Press.

Marx, Karl

    1997. *The Marx Reader*. C. Pierson, ed. Cambridge, UK: Polity.

Marx, Werner L.

    1980. *Un pueblo que canta: Historia de las iglesias evangélicas moravas en la república de Honduras*. Cocobila, Honduras: Administracion Iglesias Evangélicas Moravas.

Mauss, Marcel

    [1922] *The Gift: Forms and Functions of Exchange in Archaic Societies*. London:
    1990. Routledge.

McClaurin, Irma

    1996. *Women of Belize: Gender and Change in Central America*. New Brunswick, NJ: Rutgers University Press.

McSweeney, Kendra

    2000. "In the Forest Is Our Money": The Changing Role of Commercial Extraction in Tawahka Livelihoods, Eastern Honduras. PhD dissertation, McGill University.

Mead, George Herbert

    1964. *On Social Psychology*. A. Strauss, ed. Chicago: University of Chicago Press.

Meltzoff, Sarah Keene, and Jennifer Schull

    1999. Miskito Ethnic Struggle over Land and Lobster: Conserving Culture and Resources on Corn Island. *Culture and Agriculture* 21(3):10–18.

Menon, Shanti

    1995. Male Authority and Female Autonomy: A Study of the Matrilineal Nayars of Kerala, South India. In *Gender, Kinship, Power: A Comparative and Interdisciplinary History*. M. Maynes, A. Waltner, B. Soland, and U. Strasser, eds. Pp. 131–45. New York: Routledge.

Minks, Amanda

    2008. Performing Gender in Song Games Among Nicaraguan Miskitu Children. *Language and Communication* 28(1):36–56.

Mohammed, Patricia

    1986. The Caribbean Family Revisited. In *Gender in Caribbean Development*. P. Mohammed and C. Shepherd, eds. Pp. 170–82. Jamaica: University of the West Indies.

Mohanty, Chandra Talpade

    2003. *Feminism Without Borders: Decolonizing Theory, Practicing Solidarity*. Durham, NC: Duke University Press.

Mollett, Sharleen

    2006. Race and Natural Resource Conflicts in Honduras: The Miskito and Garífuna Struggle for Lasa Pulan. *Latin American Research Review* 41(1):76–101.

Murphy, Robert

    1956. Matrilocality and Patrilineality in Mundurucu Society. *American Anthropologist* 58(3):414–34.

Naylor, Robert A.

    1989. *Penny Ante Imperialism: The Mosquito Shore and the Bay of Honduras, 1600–1914: A Case Study in British Informal Empire.* London: Associated University Press.

Newson, Linda

    1986. *The Cost of Conquest: Indian Decline in Honduras Under Spanish Rule.* Boulder: Westview.

Nietschmann, Bernard

    1973. *Between Land and Water: The Subsistence Ecology of the Miskito Indians, Eastern Nicaragua.* New York: Seminar.

    1974. When the Turtle Collapses, the World Ends. *Natural History* 83(6):34–43.

    1989. *The Unknown War: The Miskito Nation, Nicaragua and the United States.* New York: Freedom House.

    1997. Protecting Indigenous Coral Reefs and Sea Territories, Miskitu Coast, RAAN, Nicaragua. In *Conservation Through Cultural Survival; Indigenous Peoples and Protected Areas.* S. Stevens, ed. Pp. 193–224. Washington, D.C.: Island Press.

Offen, Karl H.

    1999. The Miskitu Landscape and the Emergence of a Miskitu Ethnic Identity, Northeastern Nicaragua and Honduras, 1600–1800. PhD dissertation, University of Texas at Austin.

    2002. The Sambo and Tawira Miskitu: The Colonial Origins and Geography of Miskitu Differentiation, Eastern Nicaragua and Honduras. *Ethnohistory* 49(2): 319–72.

Olien, Michael D.

    1983. The Miskito Kings and the Line of Succession. *Journal of Anthropological Research* 39:198–241.

    1989. Were the Miskitu Indians Black? Ethnicity, Politics, and Plagiarism in the Mid-Nineteenth Century. *Nieuwe West-Indische Gids* 62(1/2):277–318.

Parsons, James J.

    1954. English-Speaking Settlements of the Western Caribbean. *Yearbook of the Association of Pacific Coast Geographers* 16:3–16.

Pérez Chiriboga, Isabel M.

    2002. Espíritus de vida y muerte: Los Miskitu hondureños en época de guerra. Tegucigalpa, Honduras: Guaymuras.

Peter Espinoza, M.

    2006. Parentesco y grupo doméstico de los miskitos: Los casos de Auhya Pihni y Santa Martha. *Wani,* no. 44:30–36.

Pim, Bedford, and Berthold Seemann

    1869. *Dottings on the Roadside in Panama, Nicaragua and Mosquito.* London: Chapman and Hall.

Pineda, Baron

    2006. *Shipwrecked Identities: Navigating Race on Nicaragua's Mosquito Coast.* New Brunswick, NJ: Rutgers University Press.

Pratt, Mary Louise
   1986. Fieldwork in Common Places. In *Writing Culture: The Poetics and Politics of Ethnography*. J. Clifford and G. Marcus, eds. Pp. 27–50. Berkeley: University of California Press.

Price, Sally
   1993. *Co-Wives and Calabashes*. Ann Arbor: University of Michigan Press.

Proyecto Nautilo.
   1993. Proyecto Nautilo para el buceo seguro y desarrollo de la Moskitia: Studio socioeconómico, laboral y de salud de los buzos: Informe de primeros resultados con conclusiones y recomendaciones. Tegucigalpa, Honduras: Ministerio de Salud Pública, Programa de Salud de los Trabajadores, Fuerza Naval (Escuela de Buceo), IHRM, PROMEBUZ.

Quezada, Noemi
   1984. *Amor y magia amorosa entre los aztecas*. Mexico City: Universidad Nacional Autónoma de México.
   1989. *Enfermedad y maleficio*. Mexico City: Universidad Nacional Autónoma de México.

Rasmussen, Susan
   1996. Tent as Cultural Symbol and Field Site: Social and Symbolic Space, "Topos," and Authority in a Tuareg Community. *Anthropological Quarterly* 69(1):14–26.

Richardson, Miles
   1990. *Cry Lonesome and Other Accounts of the Anthropologists' Project*. Albany: State University of New York Press.

Romanucci-Ross, Lola
   1993. *Conflict, Violence, and Morality in a Mexican Village*. Chicago: University of Chicago Press.

Rosenbaum, Brenda
   1996. Women and Gender in Mesoamerica. In *The Legacy of Mesoamerica: History and Culture of Native American Civilization*. R. Carmack, J. Gasco, and G. Gossen, eds. Pp. 321–52. Upper Saddle River, NJ: Prentice Hall.

Safa, Helen
   1995. *The Myth of the Male Breadwinner: Women and Industrialization in the Caribbean*. Boulder, CO: Westview.
   2005. The Matrifocal Family and Patriarchal Ideology in Cuba and the Caribbean. *Journal of Latin American Anthropology* 10(2):314–38.

Salamanca, Danilo
   1988. Elementos de gramática del miskitu. PhD dissertation, Massachusetts Institute of Technology.

Sammons, Kay, and Joel Sherzer
   2000. *Translating Native Latin American Verbal Art: Ethnopoetics and Ethnography of Speaking*. Washington, D.C.: Smithsonian Institution Press.

Sanday, Peggy Reeves
   2002. *Women at the Center: Life in a Modern Matriarchy*. Ithaca, NY: Cornell University Press.

Scheper-Hughes, Nancy
    1992. *Death Without Weeping: The Violence of Everyday Life in Brazil*. Berkeley: University of California Press.

Scott, James
    1992. *Domination and the Arts of Resistance: Hidden Transcripts*. 2nd edition. New Haven, CT: Yale University Press.

Scott, Parry
    1995. Matrifocal Males: Gender, Perception, and Experience of the Domestic Domain in Brazil. In *Gender, Kinship, Power: A Comparative and Interdisciplinary History*. M. Maynes, A. Waltner, B. Soland, and U. Strasser, eds. Pp. 149–74. New York: Routledge.

Shostak, Marjorie.
    1981. *Nisa: The Life and Words of a !Kung Woman*. Cambridge: Harvard University Press.

Siskind, Janet
    1973. *To Hunt in the Morning*. London: Oxford University Press.

Smith, Raymond T.
    1956. *The Negro Family in British Guiana: Family Structure and Social Status in the Villages*. London: Routledge and Kegan Paul.
    1973. The Matrifocal Family. In *The Character of Kinship*. Jack Goody, ed. Pp. 121–44. London: Cambridge University Press.
    1996. *The Matrifocal Family: Power, Pluralism, and Politics*. New York: Routledge.

Stacey, Judith
    1988. Can There Be a Feminist Ethnography? *Women's Studies International Forum* 11(1):21–27.

Stack, Carol
    1974. *All Our Kin: Strategies for Survival in a Black Community*. New York: Harper and Row.

Stephen, Lynn
    2007. *Transborder Lives: Indigenous Oaxacans in Mexico, California, and Oregon*. Durham, NC: Duke University Press.

Strathern, Marilyn
    2005. Missing Men. *American Ethnologist* 32(1):28–29.

Tanner, Nancy
    1974. Matrifocality in Indonesia and Africa and Among Black Americans. In *Women, Culture, and Society*. M. Z. Rosaldo and L. Lamphere, eds. Pp. 129–56. Stanford, CA: Stanford University Press.

Taylor, Douglas M.
    1951. *The Black Carib of British Honduras*. Publications in Anthropology, no. 17. New York: Viking Fund.

Tice, Karin
    1995. *Kuna Crafts, Gender, and the Global Economy*. Austin: University of Texas Press.

Tillman, Benjamin F.
2004. La influencia morava en el paisaje de la mosquitia hondureña. Tegucigalpa, Honduras: Editorial Guaymuras.

Tsing, Ana
2000. The Global Situation. *Cultural Anthropology* 15(3):327–60.

Twinam, Ann
2001. *Public Lives, Private Secrets: Gender, Honor, Sexuality, and Illegitimacy in Colonial Spanish America.* Stanford, CA: Stanford University Press.

Vilas, Carlos M.
1989. *State, Class, and Ethnicity in Nicaragua: Capitalist Modernization and Revolutionary Change on the Atlantic Coast.* Boulder, CO: Lynne Rienner.

Visweswaran, Kamala
1997. Histories of Feminist Ethnography. *Annual Review of Anthropology* 26:591–621.

Wade, Peter
1997. *Race and Ethnicity in Latin America.* London: Pluto Press.

Wekker, Gloria
2006. *The Politics of Passion: Women's Sexual Culture in the Afro-Surinamese Diaspora.* New York: Columbia University Press.

West, Robert C., and John P. Augelli
1989. *Middle America: Its Lands and Peoples.* Upper Saddle River, NJ: Prentice-Hall.

World Bank
1999. The Lobster Fishery of the Honduran and Nicaraguan Moskitia: A Study of the Resource, Its Sustainable Exploitation and the Problems of the Miskitu Divers Working in the Fishery. Prepared by Arcadis Euroconsult, Arhem, Netherlands, for the World Bank. Accessed November 16, 2011. http://www.docstoc.com/docs/48709922/THE-LOBSTER-FISHERY-high-margin-pharmacies.

Wright, Pamela
1995. The Timely Significance of Supernatural Mothers or Exemplary Daughters: The Metonymy of Identity in History. In *Articulating Hidden Histories: Exploring the Influence of Eric R. Wolf.* J. Schneider and R. Rapp, eds. Pp. 243–61. Berkeley: University of California Press.

Yelvington, Kevin A.
1995. *Producing Power: Ethnicity, Gender, and Class in a Caribbean Workplace.* Philadelphia: Temple University Press.
2001. Patterns of "Race," Ethnicity, Class, and Nationalism. In *Understanding Contemporary Latin America.* Richard S. Hillman, ed. Pp. 229–61. Boulder, CO: Lynne Rienner.
2006. (ed.). *Afro-Atlantic Dialogues: Anthropology in the Diaspora.* School of American Research Advanced Seminar Series. Santa Fe, NM: School of American Research Press.

Index

Abduction, Rape, and Murder, 143–44.
   See spirit possession
Abu-Lughod, Lila, 54, 169n9
Adams, Rachel, 111
ai lihkan, 172
amia tikaia, 172. *See* memory eraser
Anderson, Mark, 34
anti-jealousy potion, 135–36, 139.
   See *kupia ikaia*
anti-virility potion, 135–36, 139.
   See *kaiura ikaia*
Asang, Nicaragua, xii, 14, 38, 40, 79–80
Augelli, John P., 153–54, 170n1
Awas, 101, 148
Awastara, Nicaragua, 14

Barra Patuco, 23, 25, 113, 167n1
Barra Plátano, 9, 23, 36, 89, 112, 172
Barrett, Bruce, 169n2
Bay Islander, 27–28. *See Musti; Isleño*
Bay Islands, 97–99, 130. *See also* Honduran
   Bay Islands
beckoning potion, 136–37. See *wauwisa*
Behar, Ruth, 54, 139
Belén, xii, 23–24, 92
Bell, Charles Napier, 39
Bell, Diane, 169n7
Bilwi. *See* Puerto Cabezas
Black Carib. *See* Garífuna
black magic, 139, 159. See Obeah;
   wauhkataya; witchcraft
blackness, 31–34
Black River, 21–23, 28, 34. *See* La Criba;
   Río Tinto
Blackwood, Evelyn, 62, 165–66n2
Boas, Franz, 110
Book Summary, 44–46
boom and bust economies: as defined by
   Helms, 38–42, 107–9; historic Plátano
   economies, 122–23
The Boom and Bust Self, 107–9
Boys to Men, 100–101
The British Presence, 21–23; and English
   language, 22
Brogger, Jan, 74
Bruner, Alton, 23

Brus Lagoon. *See* Brus Lakun
Brus Laguna. *See* Brus Lagoon; Brus Lakun
Brus Lakun, 2, 25, 116, 140, 164n7
buccaneer, 39, 43, 169
Butler, Judith, 165n2
buzo, 172. *See* lobster diver. See also
   cayuquero

canoeman, 72, 84, 98–101, 105, 117, 123, 173.
   See *cayuquero*
Cape Gracias a Dios, 14, 19, 21
Caribbean Cultural Practices, 158–60
Cash-Oriented Obsessions, 89–91, 167n1
Catholic Church, in colonial era, 155
cayuquero, 173. *See* canoeman. See also *buzo*
Central American Caribbean lowlands, 21,
   154, 170n1
Central American Gender Ideologies, 153–55
Chevannes, Barry, 129, 139
circum-Caribbean culture area, 154, 160
coastal villages: everyday life in, 1–7, 13–14,
   47–52; settlement history 23–24
cocaine, 95, 102, 104–6, 111, 113, 162. See *labsta pihni*
Cocobila, xii, 1, 23–24, 115, 155
Coehlo, Roy, 169n8
COHDEFOR, 163n4
colonial Miskitu, 21–22; and British
   Protectorate, 22; natural resources and
   trade, 23; Tawira, 28; Zambos-Mosquitos,
   21, 22, 26, 28, 35, 163n1
comanche, 173. See also *buzo*
commodification of identities, 16, 41–44, 47,
   88, 97, 123, 127, 129, 138, 140–42, 153, 157–59
Conflict and Divorce, 75–76
conflict and jealousy, 76–79, 167n2, 168n7
conservative cultural core, 39, 63, 159. *See
   also* Helms, Mary
conspicuous consumption, 110–13, 123. See
   also *vagando*
consumerism, 13–14, 15, 40–41, 128–29, 159,
   161
contradictory gender and power relations,
   58, 96, 130–31, 156
Contra war, 26
Conzemius, Eduard, 19, 39, 140

migrant wage labor, 38–39, 107, 136, 159
Mikitrik, 144
misbara, 175. *See* hate potion
miscegenation: Colonial Miskitu, 19; Miskitu with Pech and Tawahka, 22, 39
Miskitu language, 19
Miskitu people: Miskito Coast of Honduras, 19–23; reincorporation, 155. *See* Honduran Miskitu; Nicaraguan Miskitu; Río Plátano Miskitu. *See also* Zambo
The Missing Men, 71–72
mixed-race identity, 19, 21, 22. *See also* miscegenation
Mohammed, Patricia, 165n1
Mollett, Sharleen, 34
monetization of identities. *See* commodification of identities
MOPAWI, 46
Morales, Modesto, 168n6
Moravian, 22–23, 45, 49, 154
Moreno, 175. *See* Garífuna
Moskitia, 19–23. *See also* The Miskito Coast of Honduras
mother-centered domestic groups. *See* matrifocal
motherhood, 15, 67–69. *See* womanhood
Motherhood Highly Valued, 67–69
mothers, daughters, and sisters, 1–14, 61–81
Musti, 176. *See* Bay Islander

natural resources, 22
neoliberal economic models, 156
New Jerusalem, 24, 36, 46, 48
New Orleans, xi, 40, 154, 165n6, 165n7
Newson, Linda, 28,
Nicaraguan Miskitu, 25–26, 28, 32–36, 105, 153; identity, 35; Honduran perception of, 164n5; population, 25
Nietschmann, Bernard, 40
North American, 34, 53–54, 146. See *meriki*
North American companies, 38
North Coast villages. *See* Settlement History of North Coast Villages

Obeah, 139, 159. *See* black magic; *waukataya*; witchcraft
Ocean Mermaids, 146–48
Offen, Karl, 28
Outside and Adopted Kin, 66–67

Palacios, 1, 21
patria potestad, 154

patriarchal gender ideologies, and the Spanish, 155–56
Patuca River, 23, 25, 101, 167
Paulaya River, 23, 25–26, 167
Paya, 176. *See* Pech
Payabila, 23, 31
Pech, 21–25, 27, 29–30, 35, 144–45. See *Paya*
Pérez Chiriboga, Isabel, 105
Peter Espinoza, Meleseo, 157
Pineda, Baron, 40
pirate, 39, 43, 169
plant medicine. *See* healing medicine
Plaplaya, 23, 32
Platubila, 23, 36–37
praidi saihka, 132. *See* Sexual Magic
Pratt, Mary Louise, 164
Price, Sally, 57, 165n8
Puerto Cabezas, Nicaragua, 40, 45, 146, 149–50, 164n6
Puerto Lempira, 25, 164n6
pura yapti, 160
purchase society, 39, 42, 109

Quezada, Noemi, 139

race: of Miskitu, 25–34; Miskitu as Blacks, 31; Miskitu as Indians, 26, 28–29; racist ideologies, 35; stereotypes of Blackness, 32, 33, 34
reciprocity, 87–89
Red Lobster restaurant, 98
reducciones, 155
resistance: market economy, 160; slavery and colonial culture, 160
Return of the Lobster Diver, 48–50
Río Plátano, 7, 23–24, 29, 36–37, 41, 74, 112, 120, 142, 144, 155, 167
Río Plátano Biosphere Reserve, 14, 24–25, 41–42, 57, 74, 102, 163n4
Río Plátano Miskitu people, 36–37
Río Tinto, 21–23, 28, 34. *See* Black River; La Criba
Rivera, Brooklyn, 164n6
riverine life, 7; life in camps, 9, 10, 12; riverine travel, 8–9
Riverine Mermaids, 144–45
Roátan, 148
Romance and the Gift, 128–30
Rosenbaum, Brenda, 139
Running Away to the Rain Forest, 54–56

sacabuzo, 176. See also *buzo*
Safa, Helen, 72, 140, 153, 156